THE
STEP-BY-STEP
INSTANT POT
COOKBOOK

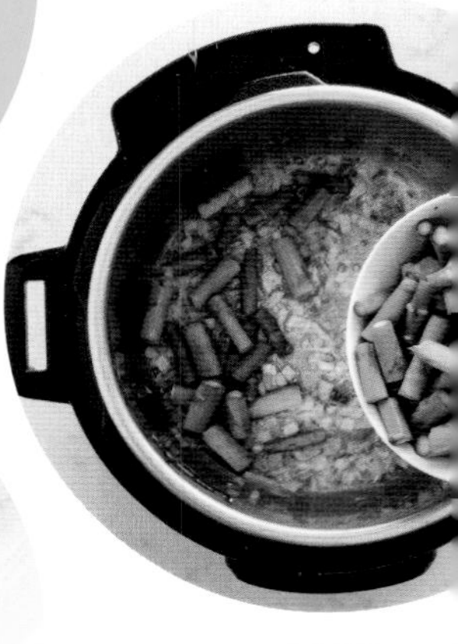

100
Simple Recipes for
Spectacular Results—
*with Photographs of
Every Step*

THE
STEP-BY-
STEP
INSTANT POT
COOKBOOK

—

Jeffrey Eisner

PHOTOGRAPHY BY ALEKSEY ZOZULYA

VORACIOUS

LITTLE, BROWN AND COMPANY
NEW YORK / BOSTON / LONDON

Voracious
Little, Brown and Company
Hachette Book Group
1290 Avenue of the Americas, New York, NY 10104
littlebrown.com

First Edition: April 2020

Voracious is an imprint of Little, Brown and Company, a division of Hachette Book Group, Inc. The Voracious name and logo are trademarks of Hachette Book Group, Inc.

The publisher is not responsible for websites (or their content) that are not owned by the publisher.

The Hachette Speakers Bureau provides a wide range of authors for speaking events. To find out more, go to hachettespeakersbureau.com or call (866) 376-6591.

Quotation from *Sunday in the Park with George,* Book by James Lapine, Music and Lyrics by Stephen Sondheim: "Putting It Together," © Rilting Music, Inc. 1984. All rights reserved. Used by permission.

Photographs by Aleksey Zozulya
Food styling by Sarah Constantino
Interior design by Laura Palese

ISBN 978-0-316-46083-5
LCCN 2019952532

10 9 8 7 6 5 4 3

LSC-C

Printed in the United States of America.

To **MOM AND DAD** for believing in me
from day one;

To **RICHARD** for being my
loving guinea pig, sampling every
new recipe I create;

And to **EACH AND EVERY ONE OF YOU**
for trusting, trying, and sharing my
recipes. You've all made me one happy
and "full"filled fella.

*A vision's just a vision
If it's only in your head.
If no one gets to see it,
It's as good as dead.
It has to come to light!*

—STEPHEN SONDHEIM

CONTENTS

Introduction

Let's get one thing out of the way. **I am NOT a professional chef.**
I'm not fancy, I cook with the most basic ingredients
(while standing over the stove in sweatpants and messy hair), and if
you told me two years ago I'd be writing a cookbook, I'd have
checked the calendar to make sure it wasn't April 1st.

In fact, I've had zero professional training—everything I've learned was from my Grandma Lil (with a little help from my mother). Grandma Lil was a remarkable and hilarious woman who could have easily headlined among the likes of Jackie Mason and Don Rickles in the Catskills, but in our family, she was famous for her cooking. My grandma never cooked with a recipe—she did it all by eye, memory, and creativity.

Enter me in 2017. I wasn't happy in my career and needed a way to express my own creativity. Then I discovered the Instant Pot, which was on its way to becoming the "must-have" kitchen appliance. Like so many others, I was at first intimidated by my new magic pot. The idea of locking my food inside, not being able to taste and adjust it as it cooked, was totally alien to how I learned to cook at my grandma's side. But I took it upon myself to learn the ins and outs of this revolutionary device. Once I had it figured out, I created my first how-to video so that everyone else who felt intimidated by it could see just how easy it is. The next thing I knew, I was developing my own recipes for the Instant Pot and posting personable step-by-step videos for each one on my website, Pressure Luck Cooking. Suddenly I was a full-time recipe creator and blogger. And now you're reading this book I wrote. Surreal!

But remember, *I am NOT a professional*. I'm just a nice Jewish boy from Long Island who loves to make delicious, home-cooked meals. So trust me on this one: *If I can cook in an Instant Pot, you can too.* If you've never cooked before but desperately want to make a great meal to impress your family (or yourself), this cookbook's for you. If you're a seasoned cook but this is your first foray into pressure cooking, this cookbook's for you. And if you're already an Instant Pot pro and just want to dig into fast, easy recipes ranging from light, vegetable-centric dishes to rich and creamy comfort food, from international to down-home favorites, and everything in between, this cookbook's for you.

I want everyone who reads this book to be able to cook along with me, just like I did beside Grandma Lil. Every recipe in this book has photographs showing you exactly what to do in each step (more than 750 of them). There are no surprises: no fancy or hard-to-find ingredients, no frilly extra steps, nothing even the most reluctant pressure cooker user can't master in moments. With me, what you see is literally what you get. And if you don't like an ingredient, just leave it out! This is cooking, not brain surgery—make what you love, and don't let anyone say you must do otherwise.

Now let's get started!

So, How Do I Use This Thing?

What I hear most often from people who just bought an Instant Pot is that they're terrified to use it. Like, to the point of leaving it in the box to gather dust (or become a perch for their cat) because they'd rather stare at it than use it.

And I get it! For some, the thought of pressure cooking *is* a bit scary. If your last memory of using a pressure cooker is from back in Grandma Lil's day, you may remember something that looked like a torture device and was liable to blow its lid off, embedding it in the kitchen ceiling. But with today's modern technology, the Instant Pot has made pressure cooking safe—and fun!

And if your Instant Pot is still in its box because you're not sure what to cook with it, here's the scoop. This appliance is a stovetop (with the sauté function) *and* an oven (when it pressure cooks). It sautés, braises, stews, and even makes yogurt, all in record time. I'm a New Yorker, so I'm always wary when things sound too good to be true (I've walked through Times Square enough to know the truth behind those "free comedy" shows), but this is one of the rare exceptions when "too good" is indeed true.

Still not convinced? Here's a quick summary:

WHY INSTANT POT?

- The cooking's done all in one pot. This means no sautéing veggies or meat in a separate pot, no straining pasta before serving, and no transferring from your stovetop to the oven to bake. Even better? Less cleanup!

- Under pressure, your food is done in a fraction of the time of regular cooking. Gone are the days of waiting 6–8 hours for a fork-tender roast from the oven or feeling nervous about leaving your slow cooker plugged in for a whole day at work. Pressure cuts that cook time down to minutes on the hour.

- Unlike ovens, which can vary from home to home, the Instant Pot is all electric and every unit cooks consistently—so if you follow the directions to a tee, you never have to worry about something being over- or underdone.

- It's mobile. Going on a trip? Take it with you! The Instant Pot comes in especially handy when camping. As long as you'll have access to a power source, you'll turn camping into glamping with the meals you'll prepare!

- It's a durable warrior. In the 20-day photoshoot for this book, I made nearly all 100 recipes in the same pot (a 6-quart Duo Plus) with *zero* issues in any regard. Not to mention, I've been using the same pot for nearly two years on the regular. If that doesn't prove reliability and quality, I don't know what does.

KNOW YOUR POT

Icebreakers can be awkward, so let's make sure you and your pot can become best buds in a relaxed way.

What Size Instant Pot Should I Get?

An excellent question. Regardless of the model you choose, the 6-quart model is the most popular and the one I recommend the most. It can cook for families of 4–8 and has room to fit a decent 5- or 6-pound roast. Even if it's just one or two of you at home, the 6-quart may prove useful for that alone, or if you wish to freeze leftovers and have enough meals prepared for a few weeks. All the recipes in this book were made in a 6-quart, but you can absolutely make all of them in the 8-quart, and most can be halved and made in the 3-quart.

If you have a larger family, are entertaining 8–12 people, or wish to make a really large 10-pound roast or even a small, whole turkey in your Instant Pot, the 8-quart is likely the one for you.

The 3-quart is perfect for making sides and for people who live solo or with one other person. While you can halve nearly any recipe to fit in there, don't expect to fit in a roast unless it's cut into small chunks.

Is There a Difference Between Instant Pot Sizes and Models?

Every Instant Pot model has slightly different preset features and displays, but they are all equipped with the important and necessary buttons I'll elaborate on shortly. Therefore, every model can make every recipe in this cookbook.

In terms of size, the smaller the pot, the quicker it will take to come to pressure as there's less volume to fill. Expect the 8-quart Instant Pot to take longer to come to pressure than the 6-quart. Also, because the 8-quart liner pot has more volume and a wider circumference, I always suggest adding in an extra cup of liquid when making a recipe in the 8-quart versus the 6-quart.

What Do the Icons on My Display Mean?

The Lux, Viva, SV, Duo, and Duo Crisp + Air Fryer models simply have a red or blue LED. However, the Duo Plus, Duo Nova, Duo Evo Plus, and Ultra have a blue digital screen.

On the top of the Duo Plus and Duo Nova's display, you'll see four icons that may light up at various times:

ICON		WHAT IT MEANS
	Flame under a pot	The pot is currently heating—this will turn on and off intermittently as it heats up and pressure cooks
	"P" in a pot	The pot is in Pressure Cooking mode
	Thermometer	The pot is in Keep Warm mode
	Speaker with an X beside it	The beeping sounds are turned off

On the Ultra and Duo Evo Plus, you'll also have a graph/timeline that displays where in the cooking process you are, either Preheating, Cooking, or Keeping Warm.

What Is the Trivet?

The trivet, which comes with most Instant Pots, is a little wire rack typically used only to rest roasts, eggs, or inner pots on while pressure cooking.

Your Lid Can Stand Upright in the Pot

See those two tabs on the sides of your lid and the two open rectangles on the sides of your Instant Pot?* The tabs on the lid slide into those rectangles, allowing you to keep your lid in an upright position while sautéing or when keeping your food warm instead of placing it on your countertop. This is a huge space saver and very convenient!

Just be sure to remember that the lid doesn't have a hinge; you must always pull the lid up to remove it from the resting position before you secure it on the pot. If you try to close it down as if it were on a hinge, you might snap off the plastic tab, damaging the lid.

This is the case on all models except the Lux, which has a slightly different lid design.

THE BUTTONS

Depending on your model of Instant Pot, you may see a number of buttons and settings, such as Multigrain, Poultry, or Porridge, to name a few. The control panel can appear overwhelming at first glance, and each model has its own configuration, but don't worry: I'll walk you through it all. The truth is, most of these presets are just bells and whistles, and you don't need to touch them to cook any of the recipes in this book. There are just a few universal buttons you need to pay attention to (the labels vary between models, but I give both names whenever applicable).

Sauté

This feature essentially turns your Instant Pot into an electric skillet or a pot on the stove and allows you to brown veggies and sear meats at three different temperatures: Less or Low, Normal or Medium, and More or High. Depending on your model, you can switch between the temperatures by either hitting the Adjust button or the Sauté button again (if your model doesn't have an Adjust button) until you reach your desired temperature.

On nearly all models, you can only sauté for a maximum of 30 minutes at a time before the Instant Pot will turn off (the Duo Evo Plus allows you 60 minutes max). Most recipes won't have you sautéing for more than 10–15 minutes, but if you do need more time, simply hit the Sauté button again to restart the cycle. Once you hit the Sauté button, give it a few seconds and it will beep with the display indicating On. That means it is heating up. (If your pot is a Duo Crisp, Duo Evo Plus, or Ultra model, you'll need to hit Start to begin the function.) When it reads Hot, that means the pot has reached the temperature you've selected. I find you do not have to wait until it reads Hot before the oil's heated—just allow about 3 minutes for the oil to heat and the butter to melt and bubble. I always sauté with the lid off, but you can put the lid on to simmer sauces or stews—just make sure the valve is in the venting position so steam can escape, or the pot can accidentally come to pressure due to the steam.

Manual or Pressure Cook

Depending on your model, there are buttons labeled either Manual or Pressure Cook, but they do the exact same thing: bring the pot to pressure. This function is not to be confused with the Pressure or Pressure Level buttons, which simply adjust the level from Low Pressure to High Pressure (all my recipes call for High Pressure, so don't worry too much about this). When you hit Manual or Pressure Cook, the display should indicate High, but if it doesn't, hit either Pressure or Pressure Level to change it.

On some models, you'll also see Less or Low, Normal or Medium, and More or High options displayed when pressure cooking. This is confusing to many (myself included). Therefore, I always use the default Normal or Medium setting.

Setting the Cook Time

Once you hit Manual or Pressure Cook, select the cooking time using the + (plus, for more time) or − (minus, for less time) buttons.

A few moments after you set the time, the pot will beep and the display will say On. This means the pot is going to begin to build pressure. (For the Duo Evo Plus model, after hitting the Pressure Cook button, select Custom with the push knob and set your cook time. And like the Evo Plus, if you have an Ultra model, scroll with the knob to set the time and then hit Start to activate the function.) The timer will not immediately begin to count down, since the On phase means it's building pressure. Once the pot comes to pressure, the pin will pop up, and a few moments later (sometimes immediately, sometimes after a few minutes) the time will appear on the display and begin to count down. Also, once the pin is up, the lid will be securely locked so you shouldn't be able to remove it until all the pressure is released and the pin drops. This is a terrific safety feature.

Speaking of which, on some Lux and earlier Duo models, the time you set will simply be the number of minutes you set it for. So if you want 8 minutes, the screen will just read 8. But if you're on later-version Duo models and any other model in the line, the

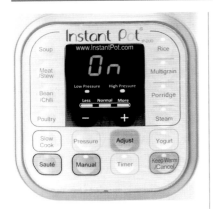

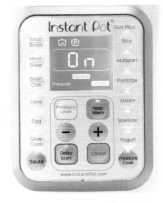

INSTANT POT DUO
(original model)

INSTANT POT DUO
(updated model)

INSTANT POT DUO PLUS

THE DISPLAY

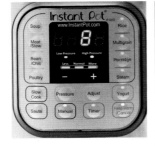

In the older Duo models, the cook time is only displayed in minutes

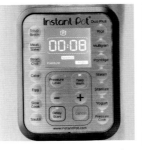

But in all newer Duos and above, the cook time is displayed with minutes to the right of the colon and hours to the left

The Duo Evo Plus and Ultra models require a push-dial to set times and functions

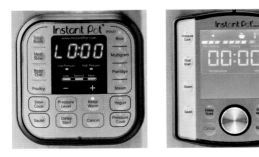

When you're done pressure cooking, the display will begin to count up, showing L0:00 or 00:00 for elapsed time

Turn your pot's sound on and off with the + and - buttons

minutes are on the right of the colon and hours are to the left. So 8 minutes will read as 00:08 and 8 hours will read as 08:00 (you'll never pressure cook anything for that long, and only the Duo Evo Plus can go that high in terms of pressure cook time).

Once the cook cycle is complete, the display will either read L0:00 or 00:00 (depending on your model) and will begin to count up by the minute showing you how much time has elapsed since. This comes in especially handy when doing a natural release (more on the types of releases shortly) so you can see when it's time to quick release the rest of the steam.

Keep Warm/Cancel

Some models have these functions tied to the same button while others have them as separate ones. The Keep Warm or Keep Warm/Cancel button should light up when you are pressure cooking so that once the cook cycle is complete, it will automatically keep the food warm. You will also hit the Keep Warm/Cancel or Cancel button when you wish to switch from one function/mode to another or to turn your pot off (it will say Off on the display when it is, indeed, off).

Delay Start

On most models, you can hit the Delay Start button and select how much time you wish to wait before the pressure cooking process will begin automatically. Just make sure the lid is secured and the valve is in the sealing position before setting and forgetting. And while it's generally fine to keep food in the pot for a few hours before pressure cooking, just make sure you don't wait so long that it's unsafe to eat. If using raw meat, stick to delays under an hour.

How to Adjust the Sound on Your Instant Pot

If the beeping sound on your Instant Pot irritates you or freaks out your pet, you can turn it off:

On the Duo, Duo Plus, Duo Nova, SV, and Viva models, while in the Off position, hit the – (minus) button and it will read SOff meaning Sound Off. To turn it on again, hit the + (plus) button and it will say

SOn meaning Sound On. The Duo Plus and Duo Nova will also show an icon of a speaker with an X next to it when the sound is off.

On the Ultra and Duo Evo Plus models, while Off is displayed on the screen, press and hold the push-button knob for a few moments and then select the desired setting by turning the knob. Press and hold the button knob again for another few moments to lock in the settings.

THE STEAM RELEASES

In every recipe, you'll see instructions on how to release the steam when the cooking's done. This means releasing all the pressure from the pot before the lid can come off. There are three possible releases: Quick Release, Natural Release, and Controlled Release.

QUICK RELEASE (OR QR): Once the cooking time is up, manually move the valve/switch on the lid from the sealing position to the venting position. All the steam will immediately release from the pot. *It's important never to put your hand or wrist directly over the valve, as superheated steam can cause a nasty burn.* Just use your finger to carefully turn the valve (or use the rice paddle that may have come with your Instant Pot) and wait until all the steam has escaped and the pin has dropped to unlock the lid.

NATURAL RELEASE/NATURAL PRESSURE RELEASE (OR NR/NPR): Once the pressure cooking cycle is complete, let the pot sit, undisturbed, for the specified amount of time so the steam dissipates on its own. For example, if the recipe calls for a 1-minute natural release, do nothing until the display reads

L0:01 or 00:01, depending on your model. If it calls for a 15-minute natural release, wait for L0:15 or 00:15, and so on. After that, finish it off with a quick release.

If a recipe calls for a full natural release, it means you do nothing until the pin in the lid drops and the lid can be opened. This can take anywhere from 5 to 45 minutes depending on how much volume is in the pot.

CONTROLLED RELEASE (OR CR): This means you'll release the steam in short bursts during the quick-release stage. None of my recipes call for this, but if for whatever reason your pot begins to spurt out foam while releasing (this can happen for any number of reasons—a starchy ingredient, altitude, etc., and it's nothing to worry about!) this is a great way to minimize any mess.

BEFORE YOU COOK

As easy as using an Instant Pot is, there are some important pressure cooking rules of thumb to ensure delicious success.

A Pot Can't Come to Pressure Unless There's Liquid in It

Though the Instant Pot may seem like magic, its inner workings are actually very simple: when heated, liquid inside the pot creates steam, which, when confined inside the airtight lid, produces the pressure that cooks your food. No steam, no pressure! As a general rule, you need a minimum of 1 cup of liquid in the pot for things to come to pressure.

Now, there are exceptions to every rule, so don't panic if you see a recipe that calls for less liquid. But if you're trying to pressure cook something with no liquid in the pot, you're going to have a hard time.

Add Cheese and Most Dairy After Pressure Cooking

One surefire way to ruin a recipe is by adding in anything too thick before pressure cooking. Thick cream or cheese can separate or curdle under pressure and may even burn onto the bottom of the pot (more on that later).

Deglaze, Deglaze, Deglaze!

When you start cooking by sautéing your vegetables or meats, as so many of these recipes call for, some ingredients (especially spices and meats) may brown and get stuck to the bottom of the stainless-steel liner pot. This is totally normal! But to prevent burning as the pot comes to pressure, make sure you're using a wooden spoon or spatula to constantly stir and scrape up these browned bits—especially once you add liquid or water-releasing vegetables such as onions. This is called deglazing the pot, if you're fancy, and it should always be done before sealing the lid and starting the pressure cooking cycle. You'll see me remind you throughout my recipes to do so, but in general: when in doubt, give that bottom a good scrape—especially before the lid is secured for pressure cooking. You'll thank me later.

 JEFF'S TIP **True story: Adding a little splash of wine or Worcestershire sauce to a pot with lots caked onto the bottom and then scraping with a wooden spatula/spoon will clear it up almost instantly. It's like magic and you'll see it often in my recipes.**

Always Make Sure the Stainless-Steel Liner Pot Is in the Instant Pot Before Using!

You just dumped all your ingredients in the Instant Pot and see everything seeping out of the bottom. You are confused at first but then realize you never put in the stainless-steel liner pot, potentially ruining your Instant Pot. Grandma Lil would shout "Oy gevalt!" I can't tell you how many times I've seen this happen to people. We're only human, but *always* make sure the stainless-steel liner pot is IN the Instant Pot before doing any cooking.

Never Set Your Instant Pot on the Stove!

Along the lines of basic human error, some people place their Instant Pot on their stovetop without realizing that a burner is warm or has been turned on by mistake. This melts the plastic bottom of the Instant Pot, ruining it. Whether in use or not, always keep your Instant Pot in a safe place on your countertop.

CARING FOR YOUR INSTANT POT

Taking care of your Instant Pot is wise and prolongs its life. After all, it's working so hard for you, you ought to show it some love in return!

If any food gets caught under the lip the lid latches on to, you can clean it with Q-tips or those tiny little foam paint brushes you can get at a hardware store. I simply dampen a brush and do a few passes under the brim. Then you can use a dry one to absorb any remaining liquid.

The lid and liner pot are dishwasher safe—just remove the steam valve/nozzle from the lid beforehand, and be sure to wash the lid on the top rack.

 Since the sealing ring (gasket) is made of absorbent silicone, it is inevitable that it will absorb the smells of your cooking. This doesn't bother me, but if it does you, place the ring in a tall drinking glass filled with warm water and a tablespoon of white vinegar and let it soak overnight. Allow it to air-dry. Or pop in your dishwasher.

It may also be a good idea to purchase additional color-coded silicone sealing rings online (they're very cheap and usually sold in sets of two or three). Use one for seafood, another for meats, and another for spicy dishes. I suggest you replace your silicone sealing rings every 6–12 months or so, as they'll wear out with regular use and can stop your pot from sealing properly.

After a few uses, your liner pot may get a bit dull and not as shiny as it once was. To me, this is a badge of honor: it shows how many delicious meals were created in the pot. However, if you want to restore your stainless-steel liner pot to the mirror-shine of the day you took it out of the box, a cleaning product called Barkeeper's Friend works magic.

When you're not using your pot, store it in a dry, room-temperature place.

FAQS/TROUBLESHOOTING

I don't drink alcohol and refuse to cook with it. What can I use instead?
A perfectly valid question (just don't invite George and Martha to dinner). While cooking with alcohol can be pretty harmless as the alcohol tends to evaporate, if you wish to omit it simply make up the difference with the same amount of broth.

My pot is filled above the max line to the brim. Is this okay?
I definitely wouldn't add liquid to reach less than about 2 inches away from the brim because there needs to be some room for the steam. Remember that as food cooks, it releases more liquid, so account for that when you use any extra space up to the brim prior to pressure cooking.

An exception to this rule is spinach, which takes up a lot of volume but ends up cooking down into nothing. Same with piling up roasts, veggies, and seafood. So long as the liquid comes no higher than about 2 inches below the brim before sealing the lid, you should be good.

Why is my pot taking so long to come to pressure?
The fuller the Instant Pot is, the longer it will take to come to pressure. If you've got a pot full with 6 cups of liquid, expect to wait between 10 and 20 minutes. If you're only making a few hard-boiled eggs with 1 cup of water, it will come to pressure in a matter of minutes. Have patience, grasshopper. The results and convenience of pressure cooking are worth it.

I got a "Burn" notice! What do I do now?
You've just put the lid on your pot, sealed it, and set it to pressure cook. And then a weird beeping sound comes from your Instant Pot and the word *Burn* lights up the display.

This can happen for a few reasons:

1 There are browned bits or rice stuck to the bottom of the pot. This is why we deglaze our pots constantly when sautéing.

2 You didn't add enough liquid. If you're using a trusted recipe like the ones in this book, you'll be fine, but be careful when setting out on your own. This can also happen if your sauce is too thick and doesn't allow steam to build up. For best results, the liquid in your pot shouldn't be much thicker than a typical soup broth.

3 You stirred in pasta (or sometimes rice) when the recipe instructions told you not to. Unless simply pressure cooking pasta in broth or water, stirring it into the liquid can clog the pot and prevent it from coming to pressure. Unless my recipe says otherwise, when adding pasta or rice to an already crowded pot, make sure you just smooth it out with a spoon so it's mostly submerged in the broth but not incorporated into it.

4 You pressure cooked with cheese or thick creams. Always stir those ingredients in after the lid comes off.

Here's how to fix it:

If the Burn notice comes on before the pot comes to pressure, remove the lid, give everything a stir to make sure nothing's stuck to the bottom, and add 1 more cup of broth or water for good measure.

If you have plenty of liquid in the pot before pressure cooking and are following a trusted recipe, sometimes there's just a lot going on in the pot—especially if it has rice with a lot of proteins and veggies pressure cooking with it. If the Burn notice comes on after the pot has come to pressure, ignore it for about 5 minutes and it should go away and resume the cook time. When the lid comes off the pot, your food will have cooked perfectly. If it doesn't go away, release the pressure, remove the lid, give the contents a stir, investigate if any food has indeed stuck to the bottom, clear it, add more liquid, and reset the pressure cook time.

Steam is escaping from the sides of the lid while pressure cooking. What gives?

Chances are, your silicone sealing ring (gasket) isn't properly seated in the metallic groove under the lid. Always make sure it is firmly in place before placing the lid on your pot. No silicone ring, no pressure.

My pot's spurting liquid during a quick release!

Sometimes this happens naturally due to altitude, how filled with liquid your pot is, or the use of a particularly starchy brand of pasta or rice. It won't do anything other than cause you to wipe down your countertop—so don't panic. Combat this by using a Controlled Release or by throwing a dish towel over the valve to absorb any spatter.

I forgot to thaw my meat or veggies beforehand!

Not to worry! You can cook vegetables, and even many cuts of meat, straight from frozen. Simply add additional time (depending on the size or thickness of the meat or veggies—see the reference charts on pages 38–41). However, I personally never cook a large roast or chicken from frozen—thawing it beforehand ensures more even cooking.

My pot's plugged in but not working!

I have encountered this before, only to realize that, on some models, the cord detaches from the back of the Instant Pot (making it handy for transport). Make sure the cord is fully inserted into the socket in both the wall *and* the back of your Instant Pot.

The pressure valve on my lid is jiggly. Is this normal?

A hundred percent. In fact, it pops off and back on for easy cleaning.

My pot seems to be about to come to pressure as the pin is about to come up, but the countdown just began and the pin's still down!

Sometimes, when the pot is filled with a lot of ingredients, it *thinks* it is at pressure just before the pin pops up. If this happens, simply press the lid down with your hands and the pin should pop right up from the pressure on both ends.

Okay, Jeff. I just took the lid off the pot and my food doesn't look super gorgeous.

Some dishes aren't going to look beautiful the moment the lid comes off. After all, the food has just been cooked under pressure, which isn't exactly traditional. However, mark my words: the finishing, post–pressure cooking touches bring about its metamorphosis into a mouth-watering, eye-candy delight.

Essentials for Pressure Cooking

Here, I'll briefly focus on the key ingredients and accessories you should have on hand for easy cooking.

INGREDIENTS

Broth/Bouillon

Broth is the base for nearly all of my recipes. Liquid is needed to bring the Instant Pot to pressure, and using broth in lieu of water adds flavor. So be sure to have plenty on hand.

My favorite for making broth is Better Than Bouillon. It is available in most markets in the soup aisle (as well as online) and comes in a variety of flavors. The best thing about it is that it's a concentrate—it costs about the same as a carton of broth, but you get so much more out of it, and a jar keeps in the fridge for a long time. Simply mix 1 teaspoon of the base with 1 cup of warm tap water (no need to boil) and you have 1 cup of broth. Where broth is called for in this book (like when you see garlic, mushroom, or clam broth, to name a few), you can almost always find a suitable flavor of Better Than Bouillon. Or, if you'd prefer to control how your broth is produced, you can simply make my healthy Bone Broth (page 30).

Cornstarch

Cornstarch is the key to giving any sauce a gravy-like consistency. Since you can't pressure cook with a thick sauce, I always cook with a thinner soup base, and after the lid comes off, a little cornstarch mixed with equal parts water to form a slurry is all it takes to thicken it right up. It's gluten free and cheap and will last you a long time. You can also substitute powdered arrowroot, potato starch, or tapioca flour instead to suit your dietary preferences.

Spreadable Herb Cheese or Cream Cheese

You'll notice I use this in a lot of my creamier recipes to gloriously set them apart. And while cream cheese is great, I prefer to up the flavor ante by using a spreadable herb-infused cheese such as Boursin or Alouette. These are the same cheese spreads you'd typically find alongside crackers on a cheeseboard at a party and can be found in many markets in the fancy cheese or charcuterie meat section. You can also usually find the spreads at wholesale clubs for a great price, usually sold in packs of three.

If you can't find or don't feel like purchasing a spreadable herb cheese, you can absolutely just use a brick of cream cheese instead.

STOCKING YOUR PANTRY AND FRIDGE

When you look at the recipes in this cookbook, you'll notice that about a third to half of the typical ingredients list is just spices and/or oils. "Now Jeff," you may think, "that's crazy! How can you expect me to buy all these ingredients?" The truth is, these spices come cheap, have a very long shelf life, and will last you quite a while since you don't use much at a time. You don't need to buy a fancy brand, either! At the end of the day, a spice is a spice—and once you taste the end results, you'll never regret the purchase. These are my recommendations.

Dry Herbs, Spices, and Seasonings

All-purpose flour	Parsley flakes
Baking powder	Poultry seasoning
Bay leaves	Rosemary
Black pepper	Sage
Creole/Cajun/Louisiana seasoning (I like Tony Chachere's)	Saffron (it's the most costly thing on this list, but you only use a pinch at a time and it lasts forever)
Garam masala (an Indian spice blend found in many markets or online)	Seasoned salt (I use Lawry's)
Garlic powder	Sesame seeds (white and/or black, toasted or raw)
Garlic salt	Sugar (white, light brown, and dark brown OR sugar substitute of your choice, such as Swerve)
Ground ginger	
Ground mustard	
Herbes de Provence	
Italian seasoning	
Kosher salt	Thyme
Old Bay seasoning	Turmeric
Onion powder	White pepper
Oregano	Zatarain's Shrimp & Crab Boil concentrate
Paprika	

Dairy, Oils, Vinegars, and Sauces

Apple cider vinegar	Low-sodium soy sauce (I prefer low-sodium soy sauce to regular since it has plenty of salt content and flavor as is. You can also use coconut aminos for gluten-free recipes.)
Barbecue sauce (I like Sweet Baby Ray's)	
Balsamic vinegar	
Butter (I prefer salted butter for savory dishes and unsalted for sweet)	
Coconut milk (always use unsweetened and shake the can to make sure it's smooth and creamy, not lumpy and thick)	Marsala wine (dry is better for cooking than sweet)
	Mayonnaise
	Mustard (Dijon, such as Grey Poupon, and yellow)
Cooking wine (cooking sherry)	Oyster sauce
Extra-virgin olive oil (regular is fine, too, but most people prefer the lively taste of extra-virgin)	Red wine (a dry one like a cabernet or pinot noir—use a cheap bottle)
	Red wine vinegar
Heavy cream or half-and-half	Sesame oil (toasted or untoasted is fine)
Hoisin sauce	Vegetable or canola oil
Honey	
Hot sauce (I like Frank's)	White vinegar
Ketchup	White wine (a dry one like a chardonnay or sauvignon blanc—use a cheap bottle)
Liquid smoke (I prefer hickory flavor, but any will do)	Worcestershire sauce

Onions

Nearly every recipe begins with an onion. Even if you hate them, you won't taste the harshness of their raw state once cooked (and they cook down to nothing). Once sautéed and cooked, they add outrageous flavor so be sure to have plenty on hand. And while my recipes call for a family of easy-to-find onions for specific dishes, don't fret. You can easily substitute one type of onion for another.

Garlic

As with onions, nearly every savory recipe in this book calls for garlic. You can get a bag of garlic bulbs and keep them on hand, or many markets have the cloves already peeled and ready to use in a little container. But if you want my advice (and have grandma cover her ears), get a large jar of crushed or minced garlic and keep it in your fridge. It saves a *ton* of time, lasts a long time, and skips the mess as you only need to scoop a tablespoon right out of the jar. No sticky fingers!

A tablespoon of crushed or minced garlic typically equals 3 cloves of garlic.

Lemons and Limes

You'll notice in some recipes that I call for the juice of a lemon or lime, either half or whole. Although there's nothing like fresh citrus, if you're using bottled lemon or lime juice instead, know that 1 lemon or lime generally contains 2 tablespoons of juice.

ACCESSORIES

Silicone Whisk, Potato Masher, and Plastic or Wooden Mixing Spoons

Since your Instant Pot's liner pot is made of stainless steel, it can easily get scratched up if you use a metal spoon to stir or scrape. I highly recommend silicone, wooden, or plastic utensils, as they'll protect your pot.

Knives

I may use magical snaps in my videos to cut things up, but in real life, these veggies and meats ain't gonna chop and carve themselves! Be sure to have a good, sharp 8-inch chef's knife to chop veggies and raw meat and a carving knife to slice cooked roasts against the grain.

Measuring Cups and Measuring Spoons

No need to guess what ¾ cup and 1½ teaspoons measurements are. These will do the work for you.

TOOLS FOR BLENDING

Let's highlight a few key appliances to make your life a whole lot easier.

Immersion (Stick) Blender

If you're making a creamy soup or pureeing a sauce, an immersion blender is one of the greatest appliances you can own. They are very affordable and will save you all the mess and effort of transferring things in batches to a blender.

With an immersion blender, you can often blend and puree directly in your pot, and just pop the blade in the dishwasher when done. Try it with my Tomato Soup (page 66) and Cream of Mushroom Soup (page 54).

Food Processor or Blender

If you wish to easily blend ingredients post-cooking that are better suited outside the pot, a food processor or blender will come in handy for recipes such as my Roasted Red Pepper Hummus (page 244) and Cauliflower Puree (page 246).

Stand Mixer, Hand Mixer, and Mixing Bowls

Every kitchen should be equipped with a hand mixer and mixing bowls. This is necessary to properly mix a cake batter like my Lemon Ginger Blueberry Cake (page 260) and even for shredding chicken (Fiesta Chicken Tacos, page 164; Buffalo Chicken Wraps, page 168; and White Queso Chicken Enchilada Casserole, page 144). In some circumstances, a stand mixer is even better—especially for creaming the batter for my Customizable Cheesecake (page 258).

It goes without saying, but be sure to have a few mixing bowls as well. I suggest a Russian nesting doll–style set so you can use various sizes to hold prepped items such as chopped veggies or cut meat before adding them to the pot.

Inner Pots (aka Pot in Pot or PIP)

Some recipes, like my Shepherd's Pie (page 204) and Customizable Cheesecake (page 258), call for an additional pot to be used resting on the trivet that came with your Instant Pot.

A few different types of Inner Pots that I suggest:

7 x 3-inch springform pan (Customizable Cheesecake, page 258; Peanut Butter Fudge Cookie Dough Tart, page 262)

6-cup Bundt pan (Meatloaf & Mashed Potatoes, page 184; Lemon Ginger Blueberry Cake, page 260)

1½-quart Corningware casserole dish (Shepherd's Pie page 204)

All can be found online, usually clearly marked to fit your specific Instant Pot's size.

Steamer Basket

A steamer basket is also a wonderful tool to help you make Bone Broth (page 30), Hard-Boiled Eggs (page 24), Premium Potato Salad (page 236), or a vegetable medley because you can easily lower it into the pot and then remove everything with the handle.

This can also be found online, in sizes to fit your specific Instant Pot.

Metal Tea Ball

As great as they are for brewing tea, these little locking mesh balls serve an even greater purpose! You can place whole, chunky spices in them, such as cloves, cinnamon sticks, and star anise, for infusing broth like in my Vietnamese Pho (page 49). You can also use a metal tea ball to easily make a batch of your favorite iced tea!

Strainer/Colander

Although we rarely drain anything after cooking in our Instant Pot (never pasta!), a few recipes call for it prior to cooking. This means rinsing grains and legumes or separating canned items from their juices. It's wise to have a hand-held wire-mesh strainer or a good old-fashioned colander to sit in your sink, when necessary.

A Few Final Thoughts

You're just about ready to dive in! Just remember, don't get freaked out. At the end of the day, this is food we're talking about here, and cooking should be fun and therapeutic. I designed this book to take any guesswork out of the game and to let you follow along with the photos for each step.

The journey will begin with basics such as Baked Potatoes (page 28) and Quick Quinoa Salad (page 30) to familiarize you with the machine so you can go on to the more exciting recipes like my Best-Ever Pot Roast (page 172) and French Onion Chicken (page 128) with no hassles or worries whatsoever.

That said, let me leave you with a few pointers.

HOW TO ALTER RECIPES FOR KETO, GLUTEN-FREE, AND OTHER RESTRICTIVE DIETS

Some of my recipes may not necessarily cater to a wide range of diets and eating lifestyles as written, but that doesn't mean you can't adjust them so they do! It's all about knowing your eating restrictions and making substitutions. If you follow a gluten-free diet, you can substitute gluten-free pasta for regular pasta (just shave off half the cook time in most cases); you can use cashew or almond milk if you wish to prepare something vegan or dairy free; you might use a sugar substitute such as Stevia or erythritol instead of sugar or honey if you're following a ketogenic diet; and you could substitute vegetable or garlic broth for chicken or beef broth if you're vegan or vegetarian—you see where I'm going with this. It is in your power to alter any recipe to fit your personal preferences.

SHOULD YOU WISH TO CRISP

While it's not at all required, some dishes are nicely finished with a quick broil. If you choose to give your finished dish a bit of a crisp, simply transfer to a casserole dish and place in your oven at 400°F or broil for a few moments.

THE INSTANT POT DUO CRISP + AIR FRYER: If you have the Duo Crisp + Air Fryer model, your pressure cooker will have all the pressure cooking functions most of the other models offer except for any presets and a yogurt function. However, that's a small price to pay since this model has the ability to go from a pressure cooker to an air fryer with the change of a lid (both are included).

If you wish to pressure cook, use the pressure cooking lid and select a cooking function to coincide with what you wish to cook. If you wish to air fry or crisp, use the crisping lid and select the crisping function and temperature at which you'd like to cook. If you accidentally put the wrong lid on, the display will read Lid, meaning you should swap it to the proper one.

This is a great way to give your food a final crisp or melty-cheese broil in your pot instead of transferring it to the oven. If you have this model, try using the crisping lid for my Tangy Chicken Wings (page 154), Maple Balsamic Brussels Sprouts (page 234), or even Lasagna Bouquets (page 97), should you wish to top them with extra cheese and finish them off with a bubbly cheese crust before serving.

For similar results, you can also use the separate Instant Pot Air Fryer Lid that will work on most existing Instant Pot models (make sure it's compatible with your model before purchasing).

AN IMPORTANT NOTE ON SPICES AND INGREDIENTS

Last but most important, my cooking philosophy is simple: to provide recipes that give you huge flavors with simple instructions. I would be remiss if I didn't equip you with the best way to make each recipe come to life in your kitchen.

That said, if you look at some of the recipes in this cookbook and think, "Wow! That's a lot of ingredients!"—it's okay! Don't feel intimidated. Most of the dry ingredients are easily accessible everyday spices, and you might already have many of them in your cupboard.

If a recipe calls for ingredients you don't have on hand and don't wish to purchase, by all means leave them out! True, your dish won't have the exact flavor I intended, but it will still taste great. There are no flavor rules in cooking—just suggestions to make it as lip-smackin' good as possible.

Now, ready. Set. Cook on!

BASICS

In this section, we'll tackle some super-basic recipes for kitchen staples that will not only taste great, but will also get you used to using your Instant Pot in no time.

Hard-Boiled Eggs & Egg Loaf
24

White or Brown Rice
26

Baked Potato
28

Bone Broth
30

Mac & Cheese
32

Garlic Marinara Sauce
34

Quick Quinoa Salad
36

GENERAL COOKING CHARTS
38

HARD-BOILED EGGS & EGG LOAF

This recipe will make you immediately fall in love with your Instant Pot. If I told you that you could make hard-boiled eggs more quickly, more easily, and so that the shell just peels off effortlessly, would you believe me? You're about to.

HARD-BOILED EGGS

Prep Time	Pressure Building Time	Pressure Cook Time	Natural Release Time	Total Time	Serves
1 minute	3–5 minutes	5–6 minutes	5 minutes	20 minutes	6

EGG LOAF

Prep Time	Pressure Building Time	Pressure Cook Time	Natural Release Time	Total Time	Serves
1 minute	3–5 minutes	20 minutes	5 minutes	30 minutes	6

8–10 large eggs

1 cup water

FOR HARD-BOILED EGGS

1 Pour 1 cup of water into the Instant Pot.

2 Place the trivet or an egg rack in the pot and then place the eggs on top.

3 Secure the lid, move the valve to the sealing position, and hit Manual or Pressure Cook on High Pressure for 5 minutes (or 6 minutes if you want the yolks a little firmer). When done, allow a natural release for 5 minutes, then quick release.

4 Place the eggs in an ice-water bath for about 2 minutes before peeling and enjoying.

JEFF'S TIP A great way to peel a hard-boiled egg is to lightly smash it and roll it on a surface until tiny cracks appear in the shell. From there, it will peel right off.

1 Spray a Pyrex bowl generously with nonstick cooking spray. Crack the eggs into the bowl.

2 Pour 1 cup of water into the Instant Pot. Insert the trivet with the handles folded down and rest the bowl on top of it.

3 Secure the lid, move the valve to the sealing position, and hit Manual or Pressure Cook on High Pressure for 20 minutes (yes, 20 minutes—anything less and you'll have an underdone egg loaf). Allow a 5-minute natural release when done (meaning you do nothing for 5 minutes once the cooking cycle is complete) and then follow with a quick release.

4 Allow the egg loaf to cool in the pot for 5 minutes before carefully removing the Pyrex bowl with some tongs or a dish cloth. Dab the top of the loaf with a paper towel to remove any condensation. Place a large plate over the top of the Pyrex bowl and hold them together. Flip so the loaf slides onto the plate, slice up, and use as you see fit—such as egg salad or deviled eggs.

JEFF'S TIP You can make as many hard-boiled eggs as will fit on your Instant Pot's trivet. If you want to make more, you can invest in a double-tiered egg tray (available online) or a steamer basket (used in my Premium Potato Salad, page 236), which will let you make as many as 18 eggs at once. The cook time remains the same.

WHITE or BROWN RICE

Nothing cooks rice to perfection like your Instant Pot. Whether you choose white rice or brown, it comes out so fluffy and perfect, you'll be making it all the time. Many of the recipes in this book make delicious, saucy dishes—and you'll want lots of rice on hand to soak up that goodness.

WHITE RICE

Prep Time	Pressure Building Time	Pressure Cook Time	Natural Release Time	Total Time	Serves
2 minutes	5–10 minutes	3 minutes	10 minutes	25 minutes	4

BROWN RICE

Prep Time	Pressure Building Time	Pressure Cook Time	Natural Release Time	Total Time	Serves
2 minutes	5–10 minutes	25 minutes	10 minutes	45 minutes	4

1 cup white or brown rice (do not use instant or Ready Rice)

1 cup water (or, for more flavor, a broth of your choice)

1 Place the rice in a fine-mesh strainer and rinse it under cold running water for about 90 seconds, shaking it around until the water coming through goes from cloudy to clear. (NOTE: Do not skip this step—unrinsed rice will be mushy and sad!)

2 Place the rinsed rice and water in the Instant Pot and stir.

3 Secure the lid, move the valve to the sealing position, and hit Manual or Pressure Cook on High Pressure for 3 minutes for white rice, 25 minutes for brown. When done, allow a natural release for 10 minutes before finishing it off with a quick release.

4 Remove the lid, fluff with a fork, and serve.

JEFF'S TIPS

If you wish to double the recipe, go for it! Just remember to keep everything in a 1:1 ratio— meaning equal parts (rinsed) rice and water. The cooking and release times remain exactly the same.

Brown rice has a slight chew to it, sort of like an al dente pasta— very satisfying and healthy!

BAKED POTATO

A baked potato is the perfect side to so many dishes. Pressure cooking these potatoes gives them fluffy centers and supple edges in half the time and with half the mess of baking them in an oven. Load these up with butter, sour cream, chives, and bacon bits if you wish, or serve them plain with salt and pepper to soak up a delicious sauce.

Prep Time	Pressure Building Time	Pressure Cook Time	Natural Release Time	Total Time	Serves
1 minute	5–10 minutes	15 minutes	10 minutes	35 minutes	4–6

1   cup water

4–6 medium Russet or Idaho potatoes, about ¾ to 1 pound each, rinsed, scrubbed, with skins pierced all over with a fork

Any toppings you wish, such as butter, sour cream, chives, and/or bacon

1 Place the trivet in the Instant Pot and pour in the water. Arrange the pierced potatoes on the trivet (it's okay if they rest on top of each other).

2 Secure the lid, move the valve to the sealing position, and hit Manual or Pressure Cook on High Pressure for 15 minutes. When done, allow a 10-minute natural release followed by a quick release.

3 Using tongs, carefully transfer the potatoes to a plate, slice open, top as you wish, and serve!

JEFF'S TIPS

If using smaller, ½-pound potatoes, decrease the Pressure Cook time to 12 minutes.

If you want an even softer potato, pressure cook for 20–25 minutes.

BONE BROTH

A good chunk of this book's recipes call for broth. Homemade bone broth is healthy, flavorful, great to have on hand for cooking, and *you* get to control what goes into it. You can either save all your bones and chicken scraps in a ziplock bag in the freezer until you have enough to make this recipe or just get some cheap scraps from the market.

Prep Time	Pressure Building Time	Pressure Cook Time	Natural Release Time	Total Time	Serves
5 minutes	**10–20** minutes	**120** minutes	**30** minutes	**3** hours	**8**

4 pounds assorted chicken or beef bones and/or scrap meat (such as chicken feet, necks, hearts, wing tips, and/or beef bones—veal or pork neck bones with meat on them also work well)

8 cups water

2 ribs celery, chopped in half

2 carrots, peeled and chopped in half

1 medium yellow onion, skin-on, quartered

5 cloves garlic, smashed

1 tablespoon apple cider vinegar

10 whole black peppercorns

1 teaspoon kosher salt

1 teaspoon poultry seasoning

2 sprigs thyme

2 sprigs rosemary

2 bay leaves

Any other seasonings you enjoy, to taste

1 Place the meat scraps and/or bones in the Instant Pot along with all the other ingredients. Stir well.

2 Secure the lid, move the valve to the sealing position, and hit Manual or Pressure Cook on High Pressure for 120 minutes. When done, allow a 30-minute natural release followed by a quick release. Allow to cool for 15 minutes.

3 Carefully pour the broth through a fine-mesh strainer with a large bowl or pot below it and discard all the solids. Now, taste the broth and season as you wish! The broth will keep in an airtight container or mason jar in the fridge for up to a week, and frozen for up to three months.

JEFF'S TIPS

When the broth cools in the fridge, you're going to see some jiggly semisolids start to appear. Don't strain these out! They're pure gelatin, which gives your soups and sauces tons of delicious flavor—not to mention great nutrients for you.

If you have a steamer basket, you can place all the items in that and lower it into/raise it out of the pot in lieu of having to strain the broth.

MAC & CHEESE

This is the very first dish I ever made in my Instant Pot. It's what convinced me that this appliance is a revolutionary kitchen tool—which sparked my whole career. You could say this recipe literally changed my life, and you'll never make mac & cheese on your stovetop again. I even give you options to up your cheese game.

Prep Time	Pressure Building Time	Pressure Cook Time	Total Time	Serves
5 minutes	**10–15** minutes	**6** minutes	**30** minutes	**4–6**

- 1 **(1-pound) box cellentani, cavatappi, or elbow macaroni**
- 4 **cups chicken broth or garlic broth (e.g. Garlic Better Than Bouillon)**
- 4 **tablespoons (½ stick) salted butter**
- 4 **cups (1 pound) shredded sharp Cheddar cheese**
- ¼ **cup grated Parmesan cheese**
- 2–4 **ounces cream cheese, cut into chunky cubes (optional)**
- 1 **(5.2-ounce) package Boursin spread (any flavor), cut into chunky cubes (optional)**
- 1 **teaspoon Dijon mustard (optional)**
- 1 **tablespoon hot sauce (optional)**
- **A few splashes milk or cream, for additional smoothness (optional)**

1 Place the pasta, broth, and butter in the Instant Pot. Stir well.

2 Secure the lid, move the valve to the sealing position, and hit Manual or Pressure Cook on High Pressure for 6 minutes. When done, perform a quick release.

3 When you remove the lid there will be some liquid in the pot, but don't worry. Add the Cheddar, Parmesan, cream cheese (if using), Boursin (if using), mustard (if using), and hot sauce (if using). Stir until it gets creamy, about a minute or two. It may appear a bit runny at first, but let it cool slightly and it will thicken up perfectly. At this point, if you want it cheesier, add in more shredded Cheddar as desired. If you want it creamier, add a few splashes of milk or cream and stir until it's the consistency you desire.

JEFF'S TIPS

This recipe allows you to customize your cheesy consistency:

- **CLASSIC AND GOOEY:** cheese-wise, add in only the Parmesan and shredded Cheddar

- **THICKER AND CHEESIER:** along with the Parmesan and Cheddar, add in either the whole Boursin package *or* 4 ounces of cream cheese

- **THICKEST AND INTENSE:** along with the Parmesan and Cheddar, add in the whole Boursin package *and* 2 ounces of cream cheese

GARLIC MARINARA SAUCE

The Instant Pot is perfect for making classic marinara sauce, one of the simplest and most versatile sauces around. My version uses a lot of garlic to really bring out the rich flavor. This is one of the easiest and best marinara sauces you'll ever have—with no sweating over a hot stove or constant stirring required. Just don't tell your nonna how you made it.

Prep Time	Sauté Time	Pressure Building Time	Pressure Cook Time	Total Time	Serves
5 minutes	**15** minutes	**10–20** minutes	**10** minutes	**50** minutes	**4–6**

½ cup extra-virgin olive oil

1 very large Spanish (or yellow) onion, diced

30 cloves garlic, 6 minced, 24 sliced into slivers

1 (28-ounce) can crushed tomatoes

1 (28-ounce) can whole peeled tomatoes

2 cups vegetable or garlic broth (e.g. Garlic Better Than Bouillon)

½ cup dry red wine (like a pinot noir)

1 tablespoon Italian seasoning

1 tablespoon oregano

1 tablespoon parsley

1½ teaspoons granulated sugar

1–2 tablespoons seasoned salt (start with 1 and add more to taste)

2 teaspoons black pepper

1 bunch fresh basil leaves, rinsed

1 (6-ounce) can tomato paste

1 Place the olive oil in the Instant Pot and then hit Sauté and Adjust so it's on the More or High setting. Heat the oil about 3 minutes.

2 Add the onion and sauté until slightly translucent, about 3 minutes. Add the garlic and sauté for 5 minutes longer, until lightly browned.

3 Pour in the crushed and peeled tomatoes, followed by the broth, wine, Italian seasoning, oregano, parsley, sugar, seasoned salt, and black pepper and stir to combine. Top with the basil leaves but *do not stir* them in.

4 Secure the lid, move the valve to the sealing position, and hit Keep Warm/Cancel followed by Manual or Pressure Cook on High Pressure for 10 minutes. Quick release when done.

5 Remove the lid and use a potato masher to lightly crush the plum tomatoes to the desired chunkiness. Stir in the tomato paste, and let stand for 10–20 minutes longer, until slightly thickened.

JEFF'S TIP This sauce will keep in the fridge in a jar or airtight container for a week, or it can be frozen for up to 2–3 months. The flavor will also really come together once it's cooled in the fridge overnight!

QUICK QUINOA SALAD

Practically every recipe in this book is incredibly easy, but this one is so basic, you could do it in your sleep (which could explain why one morning there was quinoa in my pot and I had no memory of making it). Quinoa is healthy and has a wonderfully light and springy texture—and it's perfect in this delightful vegan chopped salad.

Prep Time	Pressure Building Time	Pressure Cook Time	Natural Release Time	Total Time	Serves
10 minutes	**10–15** minutes	**1** minute	**10** minutes	**35** minutes	**4**

2 cups quinoa

2 cups vegetable or chicken broth

1 (15-ounce) can chickpeas, drained and rinsed

1 cup flat-leaf parsley, chopped

1 cucumber, diced

1 red bell pepper, diced

1 red onion, diced

3 cloves garlic, minced

1 teaspoon seasoned salt

Juice of 2 lemons

¼ cup extra-virgin olive oil

2 tablespoons red wine vinegar

1–2 cups crumbled feta cheese (optional)

Salt and pepper to taste

1 Rinse the quinoa in a fine-mesh strainer under cold water for 90 seconds and then place it and the broth in the Instant Pot and stir.

2 Secure the lid, move the valve to the sealing position, and hit Manual or Pressure Cook on High Pressure for 1 minute. When done, allow a 10-minute natural release, followed by a quick release.

3 Immediately fluff the quinoa with a fork and let cool for 10 minutes.

4 Transfer to a serving bowl and toss together with all the salad ingredients.

JEFF'S TIP If you don't feel like making the salad, feel free to season and use the quinoa any way you wish.

GENERAL COOKING CHARTS

Here's the part where I play scientist and you get a quick and general reference section on how long to cook what as well as general liquid-to-food ratios. But it is key to keep in mind these are merely suggestions, as the dish or sauce you're making may use slightly altered ratios and times.

PASTA

Pasta	Grain:Liquid Ratio by Pound:Cup	Pressure Cook Time at High Pressure	Release
Short pasta (such as macaroni, rigatoni, penne, ziti, farfalle, rotini, cavatappi, cellentani, campanelle, medium shells)	1:4	6 minutes	Quick
Linguine or egg noodles	1:4	6 minutes	Quick
Spaghetti	1:4	8 minutes	Quick
Bucatini	1:4	12 minutes	Quick

- *If making whole-wheat pasta, cut the package's suggested minimum cook time in half, and shave off 1 minute more for softer pasta or 2 minutes more for al dente pasta. If making a gluten-free pasta, cut the suggested Pressure Cook time in half.*
- *If making pasta without a sauce, drain the excess liquid before serving.*
- *If using a long noodle such as spaghetti or linguine, you must break it in half before adding to the pot. True, some Italian grandmothers may chase you with their rolling pins for doing so, but if you don't, it won't fit or cook properly.*
- *Always add 2 tablespoons of butter or oil to the pot to prevent sticking and foaming.*

GRAINS

Grain (all rinsed for 90 seconds)	Grain:Liquid Ratio by Cup:Cup	Pressure Cook Time at High Pressure	Release
White rice (jasmine, basmati, or long grain)	1:1	3 minutes	10-minute natural followed by quick
Brown rice	1:1	18 minutes	5-minute natural followed by quick
Arborio rice (risotto)	1:2	6 minutes	Quick
Wild rice	1:2	25 minutes	15-minute natural followed by quick
Quinoa	1:1	1 minute	10-minute natural followed by quick
Barley	1:1½	15 minutes	10-minute natural followed by quick
Couscous (not quick cooking)	1:2½	6 minutes	Quick
Polenta (not quick cooking)	1:4	9 minutes	Quick
Oats (steel cut)	1:2	3 minutes	15-minute natural followed by quick

- *Cook your grains in broth instead of water to really enhance the flavor!*

POULTRY

Meat (2–4 pounds)	Pressure Cook Time at High Pressure with 1 cup of liquid and meat resting on trivet	Release
Breasts, 1 inch thick, whole	12 minutes	Quick
Breasts, ¼ inch thick	8 minutes	Quick
Breasts, cut into bite-size pieces	5 minutes	Quick
Thighs, whole, bone-in or out	8 minutes	Quick
Thighs, cut into bite-size pieces, bone-in or out	5 minutes	Quick
Drumsticks	6 minutes	Quick
Chicken, whole	25 minutes	15-minute natural followed by quick
Duck breast, leg, confit	10 minutes	5-minute natural followed by quick
Duck, whole	30 minutes	15-minute natural followed by quick
Turkey, whole	40–50 minutes	12-minute natural followed by quick
Turkey breast	35 minutes	12-minute natural followed by quick

- All cook times are the suggested general times and will vary based on the quality of the cut of meat used as well as the dish you are using it in.
- If meat is frozen, add 10–15 minutes of cook time. If cooking a whole chicken or turkey, thaw before cooking.

SEAFOOD

Seafood (1–3 pounds)	Pressure Cook Time at High Pressure with 1 cup of liquid and seafood resting on trivet	Release
Salmon	4 minutes	Quick
Any other fish (halibut, cod, mahi mahi, haddock, tilapia), ¼–1-inch thick	3 minutes	Quick
Large/jumbo shrimp, tail on	0 minutes	Quick
Lobster tail	4 minutes	Quick
Snow crab legs	2 minutes	Quick
King crab legs	3 minutes	Quick
Mussels, fresh	2 minutes	Quick
Clams, fresh	2 minutes	Quick

- All cook times are the suggested general times and will vary based on the quality of the seafood used as well as the dish you are using it in.
- If using frozen seafood, increase Pressure Cook Time by 1 minute for shrimp and 2 minutes for all else.

MEAT

Meat (3–6 pounds)	Pressure Cook Time at High Pressure with 1 cup of liquid and meat resting on trivet	Release
Beef roast, whole (chuck, bottom, rump, round, brisket)	60–75 minutes	15-minute natural followed by quick
Beef roast, cut into bite-size pieces (chuck, bottom, rump, round, brisket)	15–20 minutes	15-minute natural followed by quick
Beef stew meat, cut into bite-size chunks	10–18 minutes (the more time, the more tender)	5-minute natural followed by quick
Beef short ribs	45 minutes	15-minute natural followed by quick
Beef spare ribs	30 minutes	15-minute natural followed by quick
Baby back (pork back loin) ribs	30 minutes	10-minute natural followed by quick
Pork spare ribs (St. Louis)	30 minutes	10-minute natural followed by quick
Pork shoulder/butt	60–90 minutes	10-minute natural followed by quick
Pork tenderloin, sliced into medallions ½ inch thick	8 minutes	10-minute natural followed by quick
Pork chops, ¾ inch thick	8 minutes	10-minute natural followed by quick
Lamb shanks	40 minutes	15-minute natural followed by quick

- *All cook times are the suggested general times and will vary based on the quality of the cut of meat used, the size you cut it into, as well as the dish you are using it in.*
- *If meat is frozen, add 5–10 minutes of cook time. For best results, always thaw a whole roast or pork shoulder before cooking.*

BEANS

1 pound, dried (rinsed and drained)	Pressure Cook Time at High Pressure, soaked in salted water for 6–8 hours before cooking. Cook in 4 cups water or broth.	Pressure Cook Time at High Pressure, unsoaked. Cook in 4 cups water or broth.	Release
Black	20–25 minutes	15–20 minutes	15-minute natural
Black-eyed peas	10–15 minutes	30–35 minutes	15-minute natural
Cannellini, great Northern, or navy	10–15 minutes	35–45 minutes	15-minute natural
Chickpea/garbanzo	15–20 minutes	40–45 minutes	15-minute natural
Kidney	20–25 minutes	15–20 minutes	15-minute natural
Lima	15–20 minutes	25–30 minutes	15-minute natural
Pinto	No point	30–35 minutes	15-minute natural
Red	15–20 minutes	25–30 minutes	15-minute natural

- *All cook times are the suggested general times and may vary based on the dish you are using the beans in.*

LENTILS

1 pound, dried	Pressure Cook Time at High Pressure, unsoaked. Cook in 4 cups water or broth.	Release
Lentils (brown)	10 minutes	Quick
Split peas (green or yellow)	6 minutes	15-minute natural

- *All cook times are the suggested general times and may vary based on the dish you are using the lentils in.*

VEGETABLES

Vegetable	Pressure Cook Time at High Pressure with 1 cup of liquid and veggies resting on trivet or in steamer basket	Release
Artichokes, whole	12 minutes	Quick
Asparagus	1 minute	Quick
Beets, the larger the more time	15–25 minutes	Quick
Broccoli	1 minute	Quick
Brussels sprouts	2 minutes	Quick
Cabbage, whole head	8 minutes	Quick
Carrots	2 minutes	Quick
Cauliflower, whole head	2 minutes	Quick
Celery	3 minutes	Quick
Corn, on cob	3 minutes	Quick
Eggplant, sliced	2 minutes	Quick
Green beans	3 minutes	Quick
Greens (collards, kale, spinach, etc.)	4 minutes	Quick
Okra	2 minutes	Quick
Onions, sliced	4 minutes	Quick
Peas (all)	1 minute	Quick
Peppers (red, green, yellow, orange bell), whole	3 minutes	Quick
Potatoes, peeled & cubed	6 minutes	Quick
Potato, whole	15 minutes	10-minute natural
Squash (butternut or acorn)	6–10 minutes	Quick
Tomatoes, whole	3 minutes	Quick
Sweet potatoes/yams	10–15 minutes	10-minute natural
Zucchini	2 minutes	Quick

- *All cook times are the suggested general times and may vary based on the dish you are using the vegetables in.*
- *If veggies are frozen, add 1–2 minutes more.*

2

SOUPS & STEWS

Nothing makes soups and stews like your Instant Pot. Not only is everything done in a fraction of the time it would take on your stovetop, but the flavors are next-level. Here, you'll find an array of spectacular soups to keep your soul warm and happy any time of year.

Chicken Noodle
Soup
44

Jeffrey's Blue
Ribbon Chili
46

Vietnamese Pho
49

Sausage &
Spinach Soup
52

Cream of
Mushroom Soup
54

Hot & Sour Soup
56

New England
Clam Chowder
58

Avgolemono
(Egg, Lemon,
Orzo) Soup
60

Beer Cheese
Soup
62

Minestrone
64

Tomato Soup
with Grilled-
Cheese Croutons
66

Chicken Tortilla
Soup
68

Lentil Soup
70

Smoky Sausage
& Bean Soup
72

Grandma Lil's
Unstuffed
Cabbage Stew
74

Beef & Barley
Soup
76

CHICKEN NOODLE SOUP

When a Jewish mother lowers her ladle in defeat and bows down to her child's version of this healthy comfort-food classic, you know that things just got real. This is the only chicken noodle soup recipe you'll ever need in your life. If you don't want to buy a whole chicken and cut it up yourself, you can ask the butcher in the supermarket to do it for you—just make sure you get a nice mix of parts, from the breast to the leg.

Prep Time	Pressure Building Time	Pressure Cook Time	Total Time	Serves
10 minutes	**15–20** minutes	**15** minutes	**45** minutes	**6–8**

- 1 whole chicken (4–5 pounds), chopped into quarters (leg, breast, thigh, and wing)
- 8 cups water
- 1 Spanish (or yellow) onion, peeled and cut into large chunks (you'll be removing it with a slotted spoon after the stock is made so make sure it's easy to fish out)
- 3 cloves garlic, minced or pressed

- 1 heaping tablespoon Chicken Better Than Bouillon or 4 chicken bouillon cubes
- 1 teaspoon Italian seasoning
- 1 teaspoon lemon pepper seasoning
- 3 bay leaves
- Kosher salt and black pepper
- 1–2 cups egg noodles (I prefer the wide ones)

- 2 cups carrots, peeled and sliced into ¼-inch disks
- 2 cups celery, sliced into ¼-inch pieces with leafy green tops reserved
- ½ cup fresh dill leaves
- 3 tablespoons fresh parsley, chopped (or 1 tablespoon dried parsley)
- 2 tablespoons cooking sherry
- 1½ teaspoons seasoned salt (more to taste)

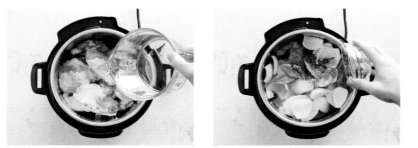

1 Place the chicken in the Instant Pot and pour in water so the chicken is totally covered. Add the onion, garlic, bouillon, Italian seasoning, lemon pepper seasoning, bay leaves, and a pinch of salt and pepper. Stir, then secure the lid and move the valve to the sealing position. Hit Manual or Pressure Cook on High Pressure for 10 minutes. Quick release when done.

2 While the pot's cooking, cook the egg noodles according to package directions and set aside.

3 When the lid comes off the pot, remove the chicken with tongs and set aside to cool. Remove and discard the bay leaves and onion (if you wish) using a slotted spoon.

4 Add all remaining ingredients to the Instant Pot *except for* the chicken and egg noodles, and stir. Secure the lid and move the valve to the sealing position. Hit Keep Warm/Cancel followed by Manual or Pressure Cook on High Pressure for 5 minutes. Quick release when done.

5 While the pot is cooking the soup, pick the slightly cooled chicken meat from the bones and discard the bones, skin, and cartilage. Shred the meat by hand and set aside.

6 Stir in the shredded chicken and serve in bowls topped with egg noodles.

JEFF'S TIP Boiling the egg noodles separately keeps them firm. Cooking them under pressure makes them absorb too much of the broth and become mushy.

JEFFREY'S BLUE RIBBON CHILI

Does your office, local fair, or place of worship have a chili cook-off? Do you want to win some serious bragging rights and *become* the place of worship? Look no further: this recipe has won my followers so many contests that it would be a crime not to share it here. If your family, team, or colleagues aren't fans of spice, feel free to skip either or both of the hot peppers.

Prep Time	Sauté Time	Pressure Building Time	Pressure Cook Time	Total Time	Serves
15 minutes	**5–10** minutes	**10–20** minutes	**5** minutes	**55** minutes	**4–6**

- **3 tablespoons salted butter**
- **1 medium yellow onion, finely diced**
- **1 poblano pepper, seeds removed, finely diced (a mild pepper; if you can't find one, use a green bell pepper)**
- **1 jalapeño pepper, seeds removed, finely diced (a medium-hot pepper; optional)**
- **1 habanero or Scotch bonnet pepper, sliced in half, seeds removed (a very hot pepper; optional)**
- **3 cloves garlic, minced or pressed**

- **1½ pounds ground beef (or ground turkey or chicken)**
- **½ cup beer (like Budweiser)**
- **1 (14.5-ounce) can diced tomatoes**
- **1 (10-ounce) can Rotel tomatoes**
- **1 (8-ounce) can tomato sauce**
- **¼ cup taco sauce**
- **1 tablespoon hoisin sauce**
- **1 teaspoon Worcestershire sauce**
- **2 tablespoons cumin**
- **1½ teaspoons seasoned salt**
- **1 teaspoon Italian seasoning**
- **1 teaspoon dried cilantro**

- **1 teaspoon celery salt**
- **½ teaspoon chili powder**
- **1 teaspoon Tony Chachere's Creole Seasoning or any Louisiana-style seasoning (optional)**
- **2 (15.5-ounce) cans red kidney beans, drained and rinsed**
- **2–4 tablespoons Chili Better Than Bouillon (optional; start with 2 tablespoons and add more to taste)**

TO SERVE
Shredded cheese of your choice
Sour cream
Oyster crackers

1 Place the butter in the Instant Pot and hit Sauté on the More or High setting. Once the butter's melted, add the onion and the poblano, jalapeño, and habanero peppers (if using) and sauté, stirring, for 5 minutes, until softened. Add the garlic and sauté for another minute. If you used it, remove the habanero pepper and discard.

CONTINUES

2 Add the ground beef and stir, crumbling and breaking the pieces up with a wooden spoon, until slightly browned but not fully cooked (about 3 minutes). Don't drain the juices—they're how the chili gets so darn delicious!

3 Add the beer, diced tomatoes, Rotel, tomato sauce, taco sauce, hoisin sauce, and Worcestershire sauce. Stir well and scrape up any browned bits from the bottom of the pot.

4 Add the cumin, seasoned salt, Italian seasoning, dried cilantro, celery salt, chili powder, and Creole seasoning (if using) and stir until well combined.

5 Add the kidney beans but *do not stir* them in. Just lightly smooth them out to rest on the top of the chili.

6 Secure the lid, move the valve to the sealing position, hit Keep Warm/Cancel, and then hit Manual or Pressure Cook on High Pressure for 5 minutes. Perform a quick release when done and hit Keep Warm.

7 Give everything a good stir and add the Chili Better Than Bouillon (if using). Let sit on the Keep Warm setting for 10–15 minutes, until warm but not scalding.

8 Serve with shredded cheese, sour cream, or oyster crackers.

JEFF'S TIPS

While this chili is absolutely top-notch, it is a known fact that the flavor of chili always *really* comes out the next day when it's had a chance to cool down in the fridge. The cold temperature makes all of the flavors meld so that when reheated, they emerge in ways that are even more extraordinary than before! You can *definitely* make this ahead of time and even freeze the leftovers.

Don't worry about the beer—it will have cooked awhile, and the kids won't get drunk. If you don't like to cook with alcohol, substitute ½ cup beef broth instead.

Need it dairy free? Substitute an equal amount of vegetable oil for the butter.

VIETNAMESE PHO

Pho is probably the greatest noodle soup you can experience. Trouble is, the traditional method calls for hard-to-find ingredients and takes hours and hours to achieve that deep, layered flavor. This recipe is going to give you all of that flavor in under one hour.

Sauté Time	Pressure Building Time	Pressure Cook Time	Total Time	Serves
20 minutes	**10–15** minutes	**7** minutes	**45** minutes	**4–6**

THE BROTH

- 3 whole star anise (not the same thing as anise seed)
- 5 whole cloves
- 2 cinnamon sticks, broken in half
- 1 tablespoon extra-virgin olive oil
- 1½ pounds chicken tenderloins or boneless, skinless chicken thighs, thinly sliced so the pieces are ¼ inch wide and about 2 inches long
- 2 tablespoons fish sauce (Don't mind its pungent fragrance—this ingredient is crucial to the pho's rich flavor, and it tastes nothing like it smells once cooked.)

- 1 tablespoon sesame oil
- 3 cloves garlic, minced or pressed
- 1 tablespoon crushed/minced ginger (I like to use Squeeze Ginger)
- 3 cups chicken broth
- 3 cups beef broth
- 2 tablespoons hoisin sauce
- 1 teaspoon seasoned salt
- 8–16 ounces dried banh pho/pad thai rice noodles (also known as "rice sticks"), either small (linguine-size) or medium (fettucine-size)

THE TOPPINGS

- 1 yellow onion, thinly sliced into rings (use 2 onions if you want more topping; this is my favorite one—so perfectly paired with the broth)
- 1 (14-ounce) can bean sprouts, drained (or use fresh bean sprouts if you can find them)
- Fresh cilantro leaves
- 1 jalapeño pepper, thinly sliced
- 1 lime, sliced into disks or cut into 6 wedges

1 Place the star anise, cloves, and cinnamon sticks in the Instant Pot. Hit Sauté and Adjust so it's on the More or High setting. Heat and toast the spices for 5 minutes, flipping midway through. When done, remove the spices from the pot, place in a bowl, and coarsely (not finely) crush with a mortar and pestle (or place between some dish towels or paper towels and pound with a mallet). Once crushed, secure the spices in a metal tea ball or spice bag. (NOTE: These spices are 100 percent crucial to the broth's flavor—especially since we're doing this pho the super shortcut route.)

CONTINUES

2 Pour the olive oil into the pot and allow it to heat for 3 minutes. Then add the onion strands for the topping and let them cook until they're a beautiful brown and slightly charred color. Remove and set aside when done.

3 Add the chicken to the pot, immediately pouring the fish sauce and sesame oil over it and deglazing/scraping the bottom of the pot. Stir constantly until the chicken is coated and mostly white (about 2 minutes, and it's okay if some is still pink—it shouldn't be fully cooked yet).

4 Add the garlic and ginger, stirring often for 1 minute and deglazing (scraping) the bottom of the pot with a mixing spoon.

5 Add the chicken broth, beef broth, and hoisin sauce and deglaze the bottom of the pot once more. Lastly, add in the locked tea ball with the crushed spices and the seasoned salt. Secure the lid, move the valve to the sealing position, hit Keep Warm/Cancel, and then hit Manual or Pressure Cook on High Pressure for 7 minutes. Perform a quick release when done, remove the tea ball (discard the spices), and stir in the seasoned salt.

6 When ready to serve, add the rice noodles to the pot, stirring to break them up. Stir often, about 8 minutes, and the noodles should be cooked to the proper consistency by the heat of the broth.

7 Ladle into large serving bowls. Top with some cooked onion, a few bean sprouts, some cilantro, a few jalapeño slices, and a lime wedge. You can also add whatever else makes you happy—that's part of the beauty of a pho!

JEFF'S TIP If you wish to have more control over your rice noodle portion, at the start of the recipe simply let them soak in a large bowl of boiled water (about 8 cups) as you make the pho. To serve, place the desired amount of noodles in each bowl before adding the finished broth and toppings.

SAUSAGE & SPINACH SOUP

This is one of the most comforting, magical soups on planet Earth. Or Mars. Sausage, spinach, and potatoes take a delicious swim in a broth so deep and satisfying in flavor, one spoonful (or a single dunk of some crusty Italian bread) will send you out of this world.

Prep Time	Sauté Time	Pressure Building Time	Pressure Cook Time	Total Time	Serves
5 minutes	12 minutes	10–15 minutes	10 minutes	45 minutes	4–6

- 2 tablespoons extra-virgin olive oil
- 2 tablespoons (¼ stick) salted butter
- 3 large shallots, diced
- 2 pounds Italian sausage (sweet, hot, or a mix), casings removed
- 3 cloves garlic, minced or pressed
- 1 cup cooking sherry or dry white wine (like a sauvignon blanc)
- 5 cups garlic broth (e.g. Garlic Better Than Bouillon) or chicken broth
- 1 teaspoon Italian seasoning
- 1 teaspoon oregano
- 1 teaspoon garlic powder
- 1 teaspoon seasoned salt
- 1 teaspoon black pepper
- 1½ pounds baby red or white potatoes, sliced into quarters, skins on
- 5–8 ounces baby spinach
- 1 (5.2-ounce) package Boursin spread (any flavor) or 4 ounces cream cheese, cut into chunky cubes
- 1 cup heavy cream or half-and-half

1 Place the olive oil and butter in the Instant Pot. Hit Sauté and Adjust so it's on the More or High setting. Once the butter's melted, add the shallots and sauté for 3 minutes, until lightly browned.

2 Add the sausage and sauté, breaking it down with a wooden spoon until crumbled, then sauté another 3–5 minutes until beginning to brown, stirring in the garlic after 1 minute.

3 Pour in the cooking sherry, let simmer for 3 minutes, and follow with the broth, Italian seasoning, oregano, garlic powder, seasoned salt, and black pepper. Stir well.

4 Add the potatoes and top with the spinach, but *do not stir* (leave the spinach right on top—don't worry if it looks like too much; it will cook down into nothing). Secure the lid, move the valve to the sealing position, hit Keep Warm/Cancel and hit Manual or Pressure Cook on High Pressure for 10 minutes. Perform a quick release when done.

5 Stir in the Boursin (or cream cheese) until melted and then follow with the heavy cream or half-and-half. Serve with some crusty Italian or French bread.

JEFF'S TIPS

You *can* skim off some of the excess oil from the sausage before serving this soup—but if you ask me, you shouldn't. It adds an incredibly deep and rich flavor!

Some prefer kale to spinach. Go for it. But now it's called Sausage & Kale Soup and the alliteration vanishes—as quickly as this soup will.

CREAM OF MUSHROOM SOUP

This be-all and end-all cream of mushroom soup will make you think you're eating at a super-fancy restaurant (and no one has to know it's actually a budget-friendly meal at home—unless you tell them).

Prep Time	Sauté Time	Pressure Building Time	Pressure Cook Time	Total Time	Serves
5 minutes	**15** minutes	**10–15** minutes	**5** minutes	**40** minutes	**4–6**

- 4 tablespoons (½ stick) salted butter
- 2 pounds baby bella mushrooms, sliced
- 1 tablespoon cooking sherry
- 1 yellow onion, diced

- ¼ cup all-purpose flour
- 5 cups mushroom broth (e.g. Mushroom Better Than Bouillon) or chicken broth
- 2 teaspoons dried thyme, plus more for garnish

- 3 cloves garlic, minced or pressed
- 1 tablespoon seasoned salt
- 1 cup heavy cream or half-and-half
- A few drops truffle oil, to taste (optional)

1 Place the butter in the Instant Pot and hit Sauté and Adjust so it's on the More or High setting.

2 Once the butter's melted, add the mushrooms, stir well to coat with the butter, and cook, stirring occasionally, for 10 minutes, pausing to add the cooking sherry after 5 minutes.

3 Using a slotted spoon, remove about 1½ cups of the cooked mushrooms and set aside.

 JEFF'S TIP Reserving some of the mushrooms gives the finished soup a bit of texture and a lot of beauty. If you prefer a totally smooth puree, you can skip that step.

4 Add the onion to the pot with the remaining mushrooms and cook for another 3 minutes, until the onion has softened, and then add the flour and quickly stir to coat everything.

5 Add the broth, thyme, and garlic to the pot. Stir well, secure the lid, move the valve to the sealing position, hit Keep Warm/Cancel, and then hit Manual or Pressure Cook on High Pressure for 5 minutes. Quick release when done.

6 With an immersion blender or working in batches with a countertop blender, blend the soup for about a minute, until it's a smooth puree.

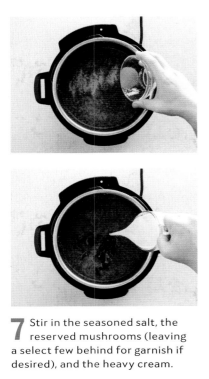

7 Stir in the seasoned salt, the reserved mushrooms (leaving a select few behind for garnish if desired), and the heavy cream.

8 Serve topped with any reserved mushrooms, a sprinkle of thyme, and a few drops of truffle oil (if using).

HOT & SOUR SOUP

This gem is a super-simple, flavor-packed Chinese-style spicy vegetable soup with all of the Chinese restaurant flavor and no hard-to-find ingredients. It may even clear your sinuses.

Prep Time	Pressure Building Time	Pressure Cook Time	Total Time	Serves
10 minutes	**10–20** minutes	**5** minutes	**30** minutes	**4–6**

- 7 cups vegetable broth
- ¼ cup reduced-sodium soy sauce
- 3 tablespoons rice vinegar
- 1 tablespoon canola or vegetable oil
- 1 tablespoon red wine vinegar
- 2 teaspoons chili-garlic sauce or sriracha

- 2 teaspoons ground ginger
- 2 teaspoons seasoned salt
- 1½ teaspoons sugar
- 1 teaspoon white pepper
- 1 teaspoon sesame oil (any kind)
- 1 pound baby bella mushrooms, sliced (or shiitake mushrooms, tough stems removed)

- 1 (16-ounce) can bamboo shoots, drained
- 1 bunch scallions, thinly sliced
- 8–10 ounces baby spinach
- ¼ cup cornstarch
- 8–14 ounces firm or extra-firm tofu, cut into small cubes (optional)
- 2 large eggs, whisked (optional)

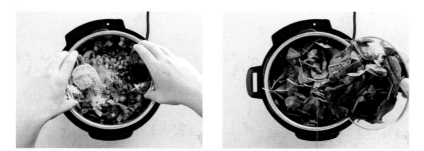

1 Place all the ingredients in the Instant Pot except for the spinach, cornstarch, tofu, and eggs. The pot will be filled to the brim (which is fine), but make sure you mix everything well before moving on. Stir well and then top with the spinach, but *do not stir*. It will seem like a lot and be close to the brim of the pot, but it cooks down into nothing.

2 Secure the lid, move the valve to the sealing position, and hit Manual or Pressure Cook on High Pressure for 5 minutes. Perform a quick release when done.

3 Meanwhile, mix the cornstarch with ¼ cup water to form a slurry. Set aside.

JEFF'S TIPS Want to use shredded chicken in your soup? Add 1 pound of chicken thighs or breasts in **Step 1** and increase the cook time in **Step 2** from 5 minutes to 9 minutes. After the quick release, pull the chicken out of the pot and set aside, shred, and return to the pot after adding the eggs in **Step 5**.

4 When the pot is done, hit Keep Warm/Cancel followed by Sauté and Adjust so it's on the More or High setting. Once the liquid begins to bubble, immediately add the cornstarch slurry, stir well, and simmer about 2 minutes, and then hit Keep Warm.

5 Stir in the tofu followed by the eggs (if using). Stir well for about a minute until little egg ribbons form before serving topped with some crispy Chinese noodles, if desired.

NEW ENGLAND CLAM CHOWDER

If you can't spend a weekend in gorgeous New England, do the next best thing and bring it to your bowl. This classic soup is full of comforting treasures in every bite. It may be a bold statement coming from a New Yorker, but this may be the best chowder you've ever slurped. The secret is the consistency: not too thick or too thin but just Goldilocks right, studded with potatoes and clams and spiced to perfection.

Prep Time	Sauté Time	Pressure Building Time	Pressure Cook Time	Total Time	Serves
10 minutes	5–7 minutes	10–15 minutes	5 minutes	40 minutes	4

4 tablespoons (½ stick) salted butter

1 yellow onion, diced

2 ribs celery, finely chopped, leafy tops reserved

3 tablespoons all-purpose flour

2 cups chicken broth or clam broth (e.g. Clam Better Than Bouillon)

1 tablespoon cooking sherry (optional)

3 (6.5-ounce) cans chopped clams, drained and liquid reserved

2 bay leaves

1 pound Idaho potatoes (about 2), peeled and cut into ¼-inch cubes

1 cup heavy cream

1 teaspoon seasoned salt

½ teaspoon black pepper

¼ teaspoon Old Bay seasoning

⅛ teaspoon Zatarain's Shrimp & Crab Boil Concentrate (optional, for extra kick)

TO SERVE

Oyster crackers

Bread bowls (I suggest sourdough if possible. You can find them at Panera, your local bakery, or sometimes in the deli section of your supermarket.)

1 Place the butter in the Instant Pot and hit Sauté and Adjust so it's on the More or High setting. When melted, add the onion and celery and cook, stirring, for 3–5 minutes, until slightly softened. Add the flour and quickly stir to coat the onion and celery.

2 Add the broth, scraping the bottom of the pot to make sure no flour is stuck on it. Then, add in the cooking sherry, all of the clam juice (but *not* the clams), the bay leaves, the leafy tops from the celery, and the potatoes. Stir well.

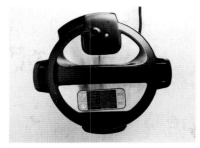

3 Secure the lid, move the valve to the sealing position, hit Keep Warm/Cancel, and then hit Manual or Pressure Cook on High Pressure for 5 minutes. Quick release when done and remove the lid.

4 Hit Keep Warm/Cancel again and then hit Sauté and Adjust so it's on the More or High setting. Add the clams, heavy cream, seasoned salt, pepper, and Old Bay (and, if you like it a little spicy, the Zatarain's) and bring to a simmer, stirring well. Once it starts to bubble, hit Keep Warm/Cancel because it's done and ready to serve!

JEFF'S TIP Do you like an even thicker soup? After you add the clams, cream, and seasonings in Step 4, add a cornstarch slurry (2 tablespoons cornstarch mixed with 2 tablespoons water), stir well, and let simmer for 2 minutes. Let thicken slightly before serving.

AVGOLEMONO
(EGG, LEMON, ORZO)
SOUP

Avgolemono, a Greek classic, is an egg and lemon soup typically served with orzo. It is heaven in a bowl—and it brings me back to my favorite Greek restaurant on Long Island, where I grew up. This soup is very thick and comforting, yet light and simple. It has only four ingredients, no cream or butter, and comes together in just minutes right in your Instant Pot.

Prep Time	Sauté Time	Pressure Building Time	Pressure Cook Time	Total Time	Serves
2 minutes	**5** minutes	**10–15** minutes	**5** minutes	**25** minutes	**4–6**

		FOR TOPPING
6 cups chicken broth	3 large eggs	Crumbled feta cheese (optional)
1 cup uncooked orzo	Juice of 2 lemons	

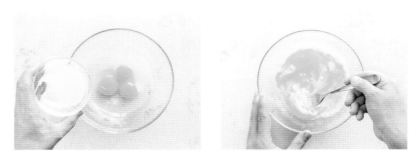

1 Place the chicken broth and orzo in the Instant Pot.

2 Secure the lid, move the valve to the sealing position, hit Manual or Pressure Cook on High Pressure for 5 minutes. While the broth and orzo are cooking, combine the eggs and lemon juice in a bowl and beat with a fork until totally combined. Set aside.

3 When the Instant Pot is done, perform a quick release. Remove the lid, hit Keep Warm/Cancel, and then hit Sauté and Adjust to the Less or Low setting.

JEFF'S TIPS Use real lemons, not lemon juice in a bottle. The fresher taste is totally worth it.

Want to add some shredded chicken? Go for it. To make life easier, toss in some precooked rotisserie chicken meat right before serving.

4 Whisking the entire time, slowly pour 1 cup of the cooked broth into the lemon-egg mixture to temper and stir until totally combined.

5 While still stirring, slowly pour the lemon-egg-broth mixture into the Instant Pot, stirring for a good 3 minutes, until the mixture looks creamy and there is no unincorporated egg visible anywhere. Hit Keep Warm/Cancel to turn the pot off, and serve topped with some crumbled feta, if desired.

BEER CHEESE SOUP

When fall rolls around, so does college football. And the only thing getting in between my partner, Richard, and the colors orange and blue and a pigskin is this Beer Cheese Soup. The hot pretzel to dip in it is a touchdown in itself.

Prep Time	Sauté Time	Pressure Building Time	Pressure Cook Time	Total Time	Serves
15 minutes	**7** minutes	**10–15** minutes	**5** minutes	**45** minutes	**4–6**

8 tablespoons (1 stick) salted butter

2 shallots, diced

2 large carrots, peeled and diced

1 red bell pepper, diced

6 cloves garlic, minced or pressed

½ cup all-purpose flour

4 cups chicken broth or garlic broth (e.g. Garlic Better Than Bouillon)

12 ounces beer (a lager or pale ale works best)

1 teaspoon liquid smoke

1 cup heavy cream or half-and-half

4 cups (16 ounces) aged sharp Cheddar cheese, shredded (since this is the key ingredient in the soup, try to find a quality one versus pre-shredded in a bag)

1 (5.2-ounce) package Boursin spread (any flavor) or 4 ounces cream cheese, cut into chunky cubes

1 tablespoon dried thyme

1 tablespoon Worcestershire sauce

½ tablespoon Old Bay seasoning

¼ teaspoon nutmeg

1 tablespoon hot sauce (optional)

Hot pretzels, for dipping (usually found in the frozen food section of most markets)

Crumbled blue cheese, for garnish (optional)

Mustard oil, for garnish (optional)

1 Add the butter to the Instant Pot, then hit Sauté and Adjust so it's on the More or High setting. Once the butter's melted, add the shallots, carrots, bell pepper, and garlic and sauté for 5 minutes, until slightly softened.

2 Add the flour and quickly stir until the veggies are nice and coated.

3 Add the broth, beer, and liquid smoke and give a good stir to combine, making sure any lumps are gone. Give the bottom of the pot a good scrape as well to ensure no flour's caked onto it.

JEFF'S TIP You can also turn this amazing soup into a fabulous fondue! Just add double the cheese to thicken and then dip in some cubed bread, Granny Smith apples, veggies, and/or chips!

4 Secure the lid, move the valve to the sealing position, hit Keep Warm/Cancel and then hit Manual or Pressure Cook at High Pressure for 5 minutes. Perform a quick release when done.

5 Add the cream and whisk in with the now-thickened broth. Then, whisk in the Cheddar and Boursin, in batches, until smooth. Follow by whisking in the thyme, Worcestershire, Old Bay, nutmeg, and hot sauce (if using) until fully combined.

6 Puree the soup by using an immersion blender or in batches in a regular blender.

7 Serve with hot pretzels and top with blue cheese crumbles and mustard oil, if desired.

MINESTRONE

The Italians sure know how to make the ultimate vegetable soup. This one is easy on the waistline, but you'd never know it from how rich, comforting, and delicious it tastes.

Prep Time	Sauté Time	Pressure Building Time	Pressure Cook Time	Total Time	Serves
10 minutes	**10** minutes	**10–20** minutes	**5** minutes	**45** minutes	**4–6**

3 tablespoons extra-virgin olive oil

1 Spanish (or yellow) onion, diced

2 large carrots, peeled and sliced into ¼-inch disks and then into quarters

3 ribs celery, sliced

1 zucchini, sliced into ¼-inch disks and then into quarters

3 cloves garlic, minced or pressed

6 cups vegetable broth

1 (28-ounce) can crushed tomatoes (I like San Marzano)

1 (14.5-ounce) can diced tomatoes

1 (15.5-ounce) can red kidney beans, drained and rinsed

1 (15.5-ounce) can cannellini beans, drained and rinsed

1 teaspoon dried oregano

1 teaspoon dried basil

½ teaspoon dried thyme

1 teaspoon black pepper

2 teaspoons seasoned salt

1 cup pipette pasta (ditalini or mini shells work well here too)

1 (10-ounce) box frozen cut green beans

5–8 ounces baby spinach

Grated Parmesan cheese, for serving (optional)

1 Place the olive oil in the Instant Pot and hit Sauté and Adjust so it's on the More or High setting. After 3 minutes, once the oil is heated, add the onion, carrots, celery, and zucchini and cook for 5 minutes, stirring occasionally, until slightly softened. Add the garlic, mix well, and cook for another minute, until fragrant.

2 Add the broth, crushed and diced tomatoes, kidney and cannellini beans, oregano, basil, thyme, pepper, and seasoned salt and stir.

3 Stir in the pasta and frozen cut green beans, and top with the baby spinach but *do not stir*—just lay the spinach on top of the broth and veggies. It will seem like a lot and be close to the brim of the pot, but it cooks down to nothing.

4 Secure the lid, move the valve to the sealing position, hit Keep Warm/Cancel and then Manual or Pressure Cook on High Pressure for 5 minutes, and follow with a quick release when done. Stir well.

5 Serve topped with grated Parmesan, if desired, and some warm, crusty bread.

JEFF'S TIPS

The soup will take a little while to come to pressure and to quick release due to all the liquid in the pot, so do be patient.

Don't want the extra carbs? Leave out the pasta.

TOMATO SOUP

WITH GRILLED-CHEESE CROUTONS

What's better than creamy, silky tomato soup with a crispy grilled-cheese sandwich for dunking into it? Having crispy grilled-cheese croutons that dunk themselves. You're welcome.

Prep Time	Sauté Time	Pressure Building Time	Pressure Cook Time	Total Time	Serves
10 minutes	**15** minutes	**10–20** minutes	**5** minutes	**45** minutes	**4–6**

THE SOUP

3 tablespoons extra-virgin olive oil

1 bunch scallions, sliced

1 yellow onion, diced

1 large carrot, peeled and sliced into ½-inch disks and then halved

2 tablespoons cooking sherry

2 (28-ounce) cans whole peeled tomatoes, with their juices

1 cup vegetable broth

2 teaspoons Worcestershire sauce

1 tablespoon dried basil

1½ teaspoons Old Bay seasoning

1 teaspoon dried thyme

1 (6-ounce) can tomato paste

1 cup heavy cream or half-and-half

1 (5.2-ounce) package Boursin spread (any flavor) or 4 ounces cream cheese, cut into chunky cubes

1½ teaspoons seasoned salt

1 teaspoon black pepper

THE CROUTONS

4 slices sandwich bread of your choice (I like rye or rye/pumpernickel swirl)

Butter or mayonnaise, for spreading on the bread and slicking up the pan

Sliced melty cheese of your choice (I use American)

1 Pour the olive oil into the Instant Pot, hit Sauté and Adjust to High or More, and let it heat up for 3 minutes. Add the scallions, onion, and carrot and cook, stirring occasionally, for 10 minutes, until they begin to soften and brown.

2 Add the cooking sherry and cook for 1 minute longer, constantly stirring and scraping up the bottom of the pot so nothing sticks.

3 Add the canned tomatoes, broth, Worcestershire sauce, dried basil, Old Bay, and dried thyme and stir well. Secure the lid, move the valve to the sealing position, and hit Keep Warm/Cancel and then Manual or Pressure Cook on High Pressure for 5 minutes. Perform a quick release when done.

4 While the soup's cooking, make the grilled-cheese croutons by heating a frying pan over medium heat. Meanwhile, spread the butter or mayo on one side of each slice of bread, and then place the butter/mayo side of the bread against the pan's surface and top with 2–3 cheese slices and then the other slice of bread on top, butter/mayo side up. Grill for 3–4 minutes and then flip. The outer edges of the bread should be a lovely golden brown. Let the grilled cheese cool for 2 minutes and then slice into 1-inch crouton cubes.

5 When the lid is off, stir in the tomato paste, using an immersion blender (or working in batches with a countertop blender) to blend the soup for about a minute or two until it's a smooth puree.

6 Stir in the heavy cream, Boursin, seasoned salt, and pepper. Blend once more before serving and top with the grilled-cheese croutons.

JEFF'S TIPS Each grilled cheese cuts apart into about 8–10 croutons. If you want more croutons, feel free to make more sandwiches.

If there's another way you like to make your grilled cheese, have right at it! But using a melty cheese (nothing's better than American) makes it much easier to cut the croutons.

CHICKEN TORTILLA SOUP

Being completely obsessed with Mexican food, I just had to include this Mexican spin on classic chicken soup. One taste and a piñata of flavors explodes in your mouth.

Prep Time	Sauté Time	Pressure Building Time	Pressure Cook Time	Total Time	Serves
5 minutes	**5–10** minutes	**10–20** minutes	**14** minutes	**45** minutes	**4–6**

2 tablespoons vegetable oil
1 yellow onion, diced
2 jalapeño peppers, diced
3 cloves garlic, minced or pressed
5 cups chicken broth

1 (14.5-ounce) can diced tomatoes, with their juices (any variety will do)
   Juice of 2 limes
2 tablespoons hot sauce
2 tablespoons salsa verde
1 tablespoon dried cilantro
1 tablespoon ground cumin

2 pounds boneless, skinless chicken breasts or thighs
½ cup sour cream

TO SERVE
Chopped fresh cilantro
Freshly sliced avocado
Shredded Mexican cheese
Tortilla strips

1 Pour the vegetable oil into the Instant Pot, then hit Sauté and Adjust so it's on the High or More setting. After 3 minutes, when the oil is heated, add the onion and jalapeños and cook for 3–5 minutes, until softened. Add the garlic and sauté for 1 minute longer.

2 Add the chicken broth, diced tomatoes, lime juice, hot sauce, salsa verde, dried cilantro, and cumin. Stir well.

3 Add the chicken breasts, secure the lid, move the valve to the sealing position, hit Keep Warm/Cancel, and then hit Pressure Cook or Manual on High Pressure for 14 minutes. Quick release when done and let the soup cool for about 5 minutes.

4 Meanwhile, use tongs to remove the chicken. Place in a mixing bowl and shred with two forks (or a hand/stand mixer for ease) and set aside.

5 Once the soup has slightly cooled, whisk in the sour cream until totally melded. Return the shredded chicken to the pot and stir.

6 Serve topped with some fresh cilantro, avocado, shredded cheese, and tortilla strips.

 JEFF'S TIPS If you like a thicker soup, make a cornstarch slurry with 3 tablespoons cornstarch and 3 tablespoons of the broth mixed together and pour in at the very end. Bring the soup to a simmer and then turn the heat off and let stand until thickened.

Want yours with beans, corn, or black olives? No problem: add them before cooking (make sure to use canned beans, and drain and rinse them before adding).

LENTIL SOUP

When a soup is simple to make, complex in flavor, *and* healthy, I'm a happy boy. Lentil soup is loaded old-school comfort food with no guilt.

Prep Time	Sauté Time	Pressure Building Time	Pressure Cook Time	Natural Release Time	Total Time	Serves
10 minutes	**10** minutes	**10–20** minutes	**15** minutes	**5** minutes	**60** minutes	**4–6**

3 tablespoons extra-virgin olive oil

1 medium yellow onion, diced

2 medium carrots, peeled and diced

2 ribs celery, thinly sliced

3 cloves garlic, minced or pressed

6 cups vegetable broth

2 teaspoons seasoned salt

2 teaspoons dried thyme

1½ teaspoons cumin

1 teaspoon black pepper

1 teaspoon dried basil

1½ teaspoons curry powder (optional, for spice)

1½ cups brown or green lentils, rinsed in cold water and drained

5–8 ounces baby spinach (optional)

1 Pour the oil into the Instant Pot, then hit Sauté and Adjust so it's on the More or High setting. Heat for 3 minutes, then add the onion, carrots, and celery and sauté for 5 minutes, until slightly softened. Add the garlic and sauté for 1 minute longer.

2 Pour in the vegetable broth and use a wooden spoon to scrape up any browned bits from the bottom of the pot. Stir in the seasoned salt, thyme, cumin, black pepper, basil, and curry powder (if using) followed by the rinsed lentils. Rest the spinach on top but *do not stir.*

3 Secure the lid, move the valve to the sealing position, hit Keep Warm/Cancel, and then hit Manual or Pressure Cook on High Pressure for 15 minutes. When done, allow a 5-minute natural release followed by a quick release.

4 Stir everything up and serve.

JEFF'S TIP If you want some meat in this lentil soup, add 1 pound of ground beef or sausage (I like Italian) and sauté with the veggies in Step 1.

SMOKY SAUSAGE & BEAN SOUP

Imagine being in the wilderness on a brisk day with a smoky campfire going and beautiful nature all around you. Now place that scene in a bowl, with smoky sausage in a rich and creamy tomato broth filled with beans that just melt in your mouth.

Prep Time	Sauté Time	Pressure Building Time	Pressure Cook Time	Total Time	Serves
5 minutes	**6** minutes	**10–15** minutes	**4** minutes	**30** minutes	**4–6**

- **2 tablespoons (¼ stick) salted butter**
- **1 Vidalia (sweet) onion, diced**
- **24–48 ounces precooked smoked sausage of your choice (I like andouille or kielbasa), diced into ¼-inch disks and then quartered**
- **4 cups ham broth (e.g. Ham Better Than Bouillon) or chicken broth**

- **3 (15.5-ounce) cans of white beans (either cannellini, white navy, or great Northern will do), divided by the can**
- **8 ounces tomato sauce**
- **2 bay leaves**
- **2 cups (8 ounces) shredded Cheddar cheese, plus more for topping if desired**
- **1 tablespoon maple syrup**

- **½ teaspoon liquid smoke**
- **2 (14.5-ounce) cans stewed whole tomatoes, drained and roughly chopped**
- **1 (15.5-ounce) can of red kidney beans, rinsed and drained (optional; for more beans and color)**

1 On the Instant Pot, hit Sauté and Adjust so it's on the More or High setting, and put in the butter. Once melted, add the onion and sauté until translucent, 2–3 minutes, then add the sausage and sauté another 2–3 minutes.

2 Add the broth and stir in one can of the white beans with the juices from the can, the tomato sauce, and bay leaves.

3 Secure the lid, turn the valve to the sealing position, and hit Manual or Pressure Cook on High Pressure for 4 minutes. While the soup is cooking, drain the second and third cans of white beans and place in separate bowls; set aside. When the soup's cooking time is complete, quick release and remove the bay leaves.

4 Use a slotted spoon to reserve 2½ cups of the sausage, onion, and bean mixture, and set aside.

5 Stir in the shredded cheese, maple syrup, liquid smoke, and drained/rinsed second can of white beans.

6 Using an immersion blender (or a countertop blender and working in batches), blend until pureed, then stir in the stewed tomatoes, the third can of drained/rinsed white beans, and the red kidney beans (if using). When serving, top with the reserved sausage, onion, and bean mixture, and additional cheese, if desired.

JEFF'S TIP

You can make this as full of beans as you wish in the final step after the immersion blending. You can also use any kind of beans your heart desires!

GRANDMA LIL'S UNSTUFFED
CABBAGE
STEW

As you may have guessed if you read the intro (and if you didn't, go back and do it), this book wouldn't be here without Grandma Lil. Her stuffed cabbage was her signature dish, so to pay her homage I've turned it into a stew that is a fraction of the work to make, but tastes identical. Legacy can be a delicious thing—and I just know she'd love this take on her classic.

Prep Time	Sauté Time	Pressure Building Time	Pressure Cook Time	Total Time	Serves
10 minutes	**10** minutes	**15–20** minutes	**10** minutes	**50** minutes	**4–6**

- 3 tablespoons extra-virgin olive oil
- 1 large Spanish onion, diced
- 2 large carrots, peeled and sliced into ¼-inch disks and then quartered
- 2 pounds ground beef (the less lean, the better)
- 3 cloves garlic, minced or pressed
- 1 (46-ounce) can tomato juice
- 2 cups vegetable or beef broth
  Juice of 2 lemons
- ½ cup jasmine rice
- ¼ cup dark brown sugar
- 1 tablespoon Worcestershire sauce
- 2 teaspoons seasoned salt
- 1 teaspoon black pepper
- 3 bay leaves
- 1 head of cabbage, cored and roughly chopped

 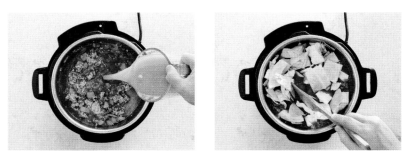

1 Add the olive oil to the Instant Pot, then hit Sauté and Adjust so it's on the More or High setting. After 3 minutes of heating, add the onion and carrots and sauté for 3 minutes. Then add the ground beef and garlic and sauté for a final 3 minutes, breaking up the meat with a wooden spoon and cooking until it is crumbled and lightly browned.

2 Add the tomato juice, broth, and lemon juice and stir. Then add the rice, brown sugar, Worcestershire sauce, seasoned salt, pepper, bay leaves, and cabbage. Stir well once more, secure the lid, move the valve to the sealing position, hit Keep Warm/Cancel, and then hit Manual or Pressure Cook on High Pressure for 10 minutes. When done, perform a quick release.

3 Let sit for 5 minutes to thicken and cool before serving.

JEFF'S TIPS

Want to make it vegetarian? Leave the meat out and use vegetable broth.

If you feel like more rice, add another ½ cup. But be warned that it will absorb more of the broth.

BEEF & BARLEY SOUP

This is a hearty and rustic soup loaded with tender meat, beautiful barley, and a classic vegetable medley. A healthy dish that's no less comforting, this will satisfy both your palate and your appetite. At the store, look for a well-marbled cut of chuck roast, with flavorful fat to melt into the soup.

Prep Time	Sauté Time	Pressure Building Time	Pressure Cook Time	Natural Release Time	Total Time	Serves
10 minutes	10 minutes	10–15 minutes	20 minutes	15 minutes	60 minutes	4–6

2 tablespoons extra-virgin olive oil

1 yellow onion, diced

1 large carrot, peeled and diced

2 ribs celery, sliced ¼ inch thick

2 pounds chuck meat, cut into 1-inch cubes

6 cloves garlic, minced

6 cups beef broth

1 cup pearl barley, rinsed

1 tablespoon Worcestershire sauce

1½ tablespoons seasoned salt

2 teaspoons dried thyme

1 teaspoon black pepper

1 pound baby red potatoes, skins on, quartered

2 bay leaves

1 Pour the olive oil into the Instant Pot and hit Sauté and Adjust so it's on the More or High setting. After heating for 3 minutes, add the onion, carrot, and celery and sauté for 5 minutes, until softened.

2 Add the beef and garlic and sear the beef on all sides for another 2–3 minutes, until the edges are nicely browned.

3 Add the broth, barley, Worcestershire sauce, seasoned salt, thyme, and black pepper, and use a wooden spoon to scrape up any browned bits from the bottom of the pot, then add the potatoes and bay leaves.

4 Secure the lid, turn the valve to the sealing position, hit Keep Warm/Cancel and then hit Manual or Pressure Cook on High Pressure for 20 minutes. When the cook time is complete, allow a 15-minute natural release followed by a quick release, then serve.

JEFF'S TIPS

The more the soup sits after cooking, the more the barley will absorb the liquid, making it even softer and the broth thicker. And to be perfectly honest, as amazing as this soup is right out of the pot, like my Blue Ribbon Chili (page 46) it's even better the next day!

To cut down on prep, feel free to use 16 ounces of a frozen vegetable medley of your choice.

PASTA

I know what you're thinking: "Pasta in an Instant Pot? Won't it get mushy under pressure?" I felt the same way at first. But then I tried making mac & cheese, and a world of delicious, al dente pastabilities was unlocked. The Instant Pot lets you make these pasta dinners all in one pot with no straining necessary. For extra flavor, my secret weapon is infusing the pasta with broth instead of water. Nonna never even needs to know...

Rigatoni Bolognese
80

Spaghetti Carbonara
82

Penne Alla Vodka
85

Linguine with White Clam Sauce
88

Sausage & Shells
90

Asian Garlic Noodles
92

Chicken Marsala Pasta
94

Lasagna Bouquets
97

Butter Chicken Bowties
99

Rotini Ranchero
102

Trippin' Tuscan Tortellini
104

RIGATONI BOLOGNESE

If I could marry a pasta dish, it would be this one. The rich meat sauce goes for a simmery swim in wine, making the aroma so addicting, it's actually romantic. After we finish it off with some tomatoes and a touch of creamy goodness? Good night.

Prep Time	Sauté Time	Pressure Building Time	Pressure Cook Time	Total Time	Serves
10 minutes	**20** minutes	**10–15** minutes	**6** minutes	**50** minutes	**4–6**

- ¼ cup extra-virgin olive oil
- 1 large Spanish (or yellow) onion, diced
- 1 large carrot, peeled and diced
- 2 ribs celery, diced, leafy tops reserved
- 3 cloves garlic, minced or pressed
- 1½ pounds ground meat of your choice (I like a veal, pork, and beef mix)
- ¾ cup dry red wine (like a pinot noir)
- ¼ cup dry white wine (like a chardonnay)
- 1 (28-ounce) can crushed tomatoes
- 2 cups beef broth
- 2 teaspoons seasoned salt
- 2 teaspoons Italian seasoning
- ¼ teaspoon nutmeg
- 1 pound ziti rigati (like rigatoni and ziti combined)
- ½ cup heavy cream or half-and-half (optional)
- 1 (5.2-ounce) package Boursin spread (any flavor) or 4 ounces cream cheese, cut into chunky cubes (optional)
- Grated Parmesan cheese, for serving (optional)

1 Pour the olive oil into the Instant Pot and then hit Sauté and Adjust so it's on the More or High setting. Allow it to heat up for 3 minutes, then add the onion, carrot, and diced celery. Sauté, stirring, for 5 minutes, then add the garlic and sauté for 1 minute longer.

2 Add the ground meat and sauté, stirring and scraping up any browned bits from the bottom, for 5 minutes, until it crumbles, releases its juices, and begins to brown. Don't pour those juices out of the pot—they add a ton of delicious flavor.

3 Pour in the red and white wine and allow the meat and veggies to simmer in it for 10 solid minutes (don't skimp on this step—it's what cooks off the alcohol and helps the meat develop that rich flavor).

4 Stir in the crushed tomatoes, broth, seasoned salt, Italian seasoning, nutmeg, and reserved celery leaves. Pour in the pasta but *do not stir,* or you may have issues coming to pressure. Simply smooth the pasta down with a spoon so it's just submerged in the broth (it's okay if it sticks up a little).

5 Secure the lid, move the valve to the sealing position, hit Keep Warm/Cancel, then Manual or Pressure Cook on High Pressure for 6 minutes. Quick release when done.

6 Stir in the cream and the Boursin (or cream cheese) and let sit, stirring occasionally, for another minute or two until everything is totally combined. Serve topped with some Parmesan cheese, if desired.

JEFF'S TIPS If you can't find ziti rigati, feel free to sub rigatoni. Just adjust the pressure cooking time to 8 minutes.

Sautéing the meat in wine is truly what makes a Bolognese a Bolognese. But if you can't tolerate it, sub out the wine for an equal amount of beef broth in Step 3. Simmer the meat in 1 cup of broth in place of the wine for 10 minutes before adding the other 2 cups with the crushed tomatoes prior to pressure cooking.

SPAGHETTI CARBONARA

Look, I'll level with you. You could be my greatest enemy, but if you showed up with a bowl of this creamy, cheesy, eggy, bacony pasta, I'd become your best friend. Until I finished eating it. Then you'd better bring over another bowl to keep the truce going. It's the best carbonara I've ever had.

Prep Time	Sauté Time	Pressure Building Time	Pressure Cook Time	Total Time	Serves
5 minutes	**20** minutes	**10–15** minutes	**8** minutes	**50** minutes	**4–6**

- 3 tablespoons extra-virgin olive oil
- 10 ounces pancetta (or thick-cut bacon), diced
- 1 medium yellow onion, diced
- ¼ cup dry white wine (like a sauvignon blanc)
- 3 cloves garlic, minced or pressed
- 3 cups garlic broth (e.g. Garlic Better Than Bouillon) or chicken broth
- 1 pound spaghetti
- 4 tablespoons (½ stick) salted butter, divided in half
- 3 large eggs
- ½ cup grated Parmesan cheese
- 1 teaspoon salt
- 1½ cups heavy cream or half-and-half
- ⅛ teaspoon ground nutmeg
- ½ cup grated Pecorino Romano

1 Pour the olive oil into the Instant Pot and hit Sauté and Adjust so it's on the More or High setting. Heat the oil for about 3 minutes, then add the pancetta and sauté for about 8 minutes, until beginning to brown. Use a slotted spoon to set the pancetta aside for later, leaving all the oil and juices in the pot.

2 Add the onion to the pot and sauté for 3 minutes, until softened and beginning to brown. As the onion sweats, add in the white wine and deglaze the pot: stir and scrape the bottom of the pot to get up any browned or stuck bits. Add the garlic and cook, stirring, for 1 minute more, then add the broth.

3 Break the spaghetti in half and add it to the pot, but *do not stir* it into the broth, just smooth it out with a spoon to make sure it's just covered. It's okay if some pieces stick out above the surface. Top with 2 tablespoons of the butter.

CONTINUES

4 Secure the lid, move the valve to the sealing position, hit Keep Warm/Cancel and then Manual or Pressure Cook on High Pressure for 8 minutes. Quick release when done.

5 Meanwhile, whisk together the eggs, grated Parmesan, and salt and set aside.

6 When the pot's done, stir the remaining 2 tablespoons of butter into the spaghetti, stirring and tossing until the butter's melted and everything is nicely combined, about a minute. Pour in the cream and nutmeg, followed by the egg mixture.

7 Hit Keep Warm/Cancel and then hit Sauté again, and it should still be on the More or High setting. Cook, stirring the spaghetti *constantly* until the cream-and-egg mixture heats through and begins to thicken, 3–5 minutes. As soon as the sauce begins to cling to the pasta, turn the pot off by hitting Keep Warm/Cancel again.

8 Add the grated Pecorino Romano and pancetta (reserving a handful for topping), and stir and toss everything until it's melded, a bit curdled in texture, and richly creamy.

9 Serve immediately, topped with the reserved pancetta and more grated cheese, if desired.

JEFF'S TIPS

Want it vegetarian? Skip the pancetta and use garlic broth in place of chicken broth.

Some like it with peas. If that's the case, add a 10-ounce box of frozen peas when you stir in the butter in Step 6—they will thaw almost immediately from the heat of the pasta.

PENNE ALLA VODKA

When a pasta has booze in it, you know it's gonna be great! But don't worry, kids, the alcohol in this recipe cooks out and the result certainly won't taste like vodka. The extra-rich and velvety tomato-based cream sauce clings to every glorious tube of penne.

Prep Time	Sauté Time	Pressure Building Time	Pressure Cook Time	Total Time	Serves
5 minutes	**10** minutes	**10–15** minutes	**6** minutes	**35** minutes	**4–6**

- **4 tablespoons (½ stick) salted butter, divided**
- **4 ounces pancetta or 4 strips bacon, diced**
- **1 large shallot, minced**
- **3 cloves garlic, minced or pressed**
- **½ cup vodka**

- **3½ cups Marinara Sauce (page 34; but look for the Victoria brand if you don't feel like making your own), divided**
- **3 cups garlic broth (e.g. Garlic Better Than Bouillon) or chicken broth**
- **1 (14.5-ounce) can diced or stewed tomatoes (go with stewed if you want it chunkier), with their juices**

- **1 pound penne rigate or mezze penne**
- **⅓ cup fresh oregano, chopped, plus more for serving**
- **¼ cup heavy cream**
- **⅓ cup grated Parmesan cheese, plus more for serving**
- **1 (5.2-ounce) package Boursin spread (any flavor) or 4 ounces cream cheese, cut into chunky cubes**

1 Place 2 tablespoons of the butter in the Instant Pot and hit Sauté and Adjust so it's on the More or High setting. Once the butter's melted, add the diced pancetta or bacon and sauté for about 3 minutes, until the fat has begun to render.

2 Add the shallot and sauté, stirring, for 2 minutes, until fragrant and translucent, and then add the garlic and sauté for 1 minute more. We don't want the pancetta to be crispy—just lightly cooked and still soft.

3 Add the vodka and deglaze for 1 minute, scraping up any bits from the bottom so it's free and clear.

CONTINUES

4 Add 1½ cups of the marinara sauce, the broth, tomatoes, and remaining 2 tablespoons of butter and mix well. The butter doesn't need to be fully melted.

5 Lay the pasta on top but *do not stir*. Just smooth it out with a mixing spoon so it's mostly submerged in the liquid (it's okay if some sticks up).

 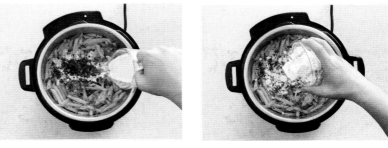

6 Secure the lid, move the valve to the sealing position, hit Keep Warm/Cancel, then hit Manual or Pressure Cook on High Pressure for 6 minutes. Quick release when done.

7 Stir in the remaining 2 cups of marinara sauce, the oregano, heavy cream, Parmesan, and Boursin or cream cheese, stirring occasionally until everything has melded, about 2 minutes.

8 Serve topped with fresh Parmesan and an additional sprinkle of fresh oregano.

JEFF'S TIPS

Don't feel like using the vodka? No problem! It just helps bring out the flavor of the tomato sauce and can be omitted.

Feel free to add some crumbled sausage, ground beef, ground turkey, or ground chicken during Step 1. But no more than ½ pound so the pot doesn't have issues coming to pressure, as it will be pretty packed as is!

LINGUINE
WITH
WHITE CLAM
SAUCE

If you've never cared for clams, do me (and yourself) a favor and just try this pasta dish. Seriously. The clams aren't fishy and just melt away into the garlic-butter sauce dressing this gorgeous linguine. And if you love clams, well, prepare to be as happy as one.

Prep Time	Sauté Time	Pressure Building Time	Pressure Cook Time	Total Time	Serves
5 minutes	5 minutes	10–15 minutes	6 minutes	30 minutes	4–6

¼ cup extra-virgin olive oil

4 tablespoons (½ stick) salted butter

1 large shallot, minced

3 cloves garlic, minced or pressed

¼ cup dry white wine (like a sauvignon blanc)

2½ cups clam broth (e.g. Clam Better Than Bouillon) or chicken broth

Juice of ½ lemon

3 (6.5-ounce) cans chopped clams in their juices, clams strained and juices reserved

1½ teaspoons dried sweet basil

1½ teaspoons dried oregano

1 teaspoon Old Bay seasoning

½ teaspoon black pepper

1 pound linguine

½ cup grated Parmesan cheese, plus more for topping if desired

1 Place the oil and butter in the Instant Pot. Hit Sauté and Adjust so it's on the More or High setting and wait until the butter has melted and the mixture begins to bubble.

2 Add the shallot and sauté for 2 minutes, stirring, then add the garlic and sauté for 1 more minute. Add the white wine and let simmer for 1 minute longer.

3 Add the broth, lemon juice, clam juice (but *not* the clams), basil, oregano, Old Bay, and pepper and stir.

4 Break the linguine in half and just lay it on top but *do not stir,* just use a spoon to submerge it gently in the liquid (it's okay if some pieces stick up above the surface).

5 Secure the lid, move the valve to the sealing position, hit Keep Warm/Cancel and then hit Manual or Pressure Cook on High Pressure for 6 minutes. Quick release when done.

6 After removing the lid, don't worry if it looks a bit soupy as that will change! Stir in the clams and the Parmesan and let sit for about 5 minutes, stirring occasionally, until the clams are heated and the sauce has thickened.

7 Serve sprinkled with extra Parmesan cheese, if desired.

JEFF'S TIPS Clams ain't your thing but want that rich garlic-butter sauce? Just leave out the clams and their juices and add in another ½ cup of broth instead. Everything else remains the same.

SAUSAGE & SHELLS

If you ever thought you couldn't make pasta and sausage in the very same pot at the same time (without draining it, no less), think again. This is my most popular pasta recipe—and was even featured on *Good Morning America*. Once you try it, I am sure you'll see why! Make sure you use grated Parmesan cheese, rather than the shredded kind, so it melts into the sauce properly.

Prep Time	Sauté Time	Pressure Building Time	Pressure Cook Time	Total Time	Serves
5 minutes	**5** minutes	**5–10** minutes	**6** minutes	**30** minutes	**4–6**

- 4 tablespoons (½ stick) salted butter
- 2 large shallots, diced
- 2 pounds Italian sausage (sweet, hot, or a mix of both), casings on and sliced into ½-inch pieces
- 3 cloves garlic, minced
- 3 cups chicken or garlic broth (e.g. Garlic Better Than Bouillon)

- 1 cup dry white wine (like a chardonnay)
- 1½ teaspoons Italian seasoning
- About 10 ounces cherry or grape tomatoes (double these if you like it extra tomatoey)
- 1 pound medium shells
- 5 ounces baby spinach
- ⅓ cup half-and-half or heavy cream

- 1 cup grated Parmesan cheese, plus more for topping if desired
- 1 (5.2-ounce) package Boursin spread (any flavor) or 4 ounces cream cheese, cut into small cubes
- 1 (14-ounce) can artichoke hearts, drained and coarsely ripped up by hand

1 Place the butter in the Instant Pot, then hit Sauté and Adjust so it's on the More or High setting. Once the butter's melted, add the shallots, sausage, and garlic and sauté, stirring, for 5 minutes, until the sausage just starts to brown but is not yet fully cooked.

2 Add the broth, wine, Italian seasoning, and tomatoes, and stir well. Add the pasta but *do not stir*. Just use a mixing spoon to make sure the pasta is submerged in the liquid. Don't worry if some of the shells are sticking up above the surface. Top off with the spinach but, again, *do not stir*. (It's going to feel like there's a *lot* of spinach in there and it will come up to the brim of the pot, but don't worry—it cooks down to nothing!)

3 Secure the lid, move the valve to the sealing position, and hit Keep Warm/Cancel and then Manual or Pressure Cook on High Pressure for 6 minutes. Quick release when done.

4 Stir in the cream, Parmesan, Boursin (or cream cheese), and artichokes until the Boursin is completely melted into the sauce. Let rest for 3–5 minutes, until thickened, before serving.

 JEFF'S TIPS A great way to slice raw sausage links easily is to pop them in the freezer for 5 minutes before slicing. They hold their form much better this way!

Want a really thick sauce? Double the Boursin to two 5.2-ounce packages or use a full 8-ounce brick of cream cheese.

ASIAN GARLIC NOODLES

This easy Asian noodle dish packs a huge wallop of flavor. Since I'm completely addicted to it, I try to keep the ingredients on hand so I can have it whenever the mood strikes.

Prep Time	Sauté Time	Pressure Building Time	Pressure Cook Time	Total Time	Serves
5 minutes	**8** minutes	**5–10** minutes	**8** minutes	**30** minutes	**4–6**

- ¼ cup sesame oil
- 1 pound shiitake or baby bella mushrooms, sliced
- 1 large red bell pepper, sliced into matchsticks
- 9 cloves garlic, minced or pressed
- 2½ cups garlic broth (e.g. Garlic Better Than Bouillon) or chicken broth

- 1 pound spaghetti
- 2 tablespoons (¼ stick) salted butter
- 2 teaspoons dried tarragon
- ¼ cup oyster sauce
- ¼ cup hoisin sauce
- 1 tablespoon low-sodium soy sauce

- 1 tablespoon ginger, minced or pressed
- 2 teaspoons chili-garlic sauce or sriracha (omit if you don't like a bit of spice)
- 1 bunch scallions, sliced, a handful reserved for garnish
- 2 tablespoons sesame seeds, plus more for garnish

1 Place the sesame oil in the Instant Pot and hit Sauté and Adjust so it's on the More or High setting.

2 Once the oil is heated, about 3 minutes, add the mushrooms, pepper, and garlic and sauté for 3 minutes. Pour in the broth and mix well, scraping up any browned bits from the bottom of the pan. Break the spaghetti in half and add it to the pot, making sure it's submerged in the broth, but *do not stir*. Some may stick up above the broth and that's fine. Top with the butter and tarragon.

3 Secure the lid, move the valve to the sealing position, hit Keep Warm/Cancel, and then hit Manual or Pressure Cook on High Pressure for 8 minutes. Quick release when done.

4 While the spaghetti's cooking, whisk together the oyster sauce, hoisin sauce, soy sauce, ginger, and chili-garlic sauce (if using), and set aside.

5 Remove the lid and mix in the sauce mixture. Let sit in the pot for 5 minutes to allow the sauce to thicken, toss in the scallions and sesame seeds, and serve.

JEFF'S TIPS Want to add some chicken? Sauté bite-size pieces of up to 2 pounds of thighs or breasts with the veggies—no need to change the pressure cook time.

Tastes **GREAT** cold too!

CHICKEN MARSALA PASTA

It's like I always say about Jews and Italians: same behavior, different savior. We use bowties for Kasha Varnishkes (Google it) and Italians use it for amazing pastas. But food knows no religion and if there's only one math lesson you need to know, it's that Chicken Marsala + Creamy Pasta = Happy Human.

Prep Time	Sauté Time	Pressure Building Time	Pressure Cook Time	Total Time	Serves
5 minutes	**10** minutes	**10–15** minutes	**6** minutes	**40** minutes	**4–6**

4   tablespoons (½ stick) salted butter

1   large shallot, minced

1   pound baby bella mushrooms, thinly sliced

1½ pounds chicken tenderloins, cut into bite-size pieces

1   (7.5-ounce) jar sun-dried tomatoes plus 2 teaspoons oil from the jar

3   cloves garlic, minced or pressed

1½ cups Marsala wine (dry)

3   cups garlic broth (e.g. Garlic Better Than Bouillon) or chicken broth

1   pound farfalle (bowtie pasta)

¼   cup heavy cream or half-and-half

2   cups grated Parmesan cheese, plus more for topping if desired

 JEFF'S TIPS Don't want to use farfalle? Feel free to use any short pasta.

1 Place the butter in the Instant Pot. Hit Sauté and Adjust so it's on the More or High setting, and heat until the butter has melted.

2 Add the shallot and mushrooms and cook for 3–5 minutes, until the mushrooms have softened and begun to brown.

3 Add the chicken and the oil from the sun-dried tomatoes (but not the tomatoes themselves) and cook, stirring occasionally, for another 2–3 minutes, until the chicken is pinkish-white in color but isn't yet fully cooked.

4 Add the garlic and cook for 1 more minute, stirring, then pour in the Marsala wine and let simmer for 1 minute more, stirring and scraping up any browned bits from the bottom of the pot. Pour in the broth and stir.

5 Add the farfalle so it's laying on top of the broth, but *do not stir*—just gently smooth and push it down with a wooden spoon so it's submerged (it's okay if some bits stick up above the liquid).

6 Secure the lid, move the valve to the sealing position, and hit Manual or Pressure Cook on High Pressure for 6 minutes. Quick release when done.

7 Stir in the sun-dried tomatoes, heavy cream, and Parmesan, and let stand for about 5 minutes, stirring occasionally, until thickened.

8 Serve sprinkled with extra Parmesan cheese, if desired.

LASAGNA BOUQUETS

With this hassle-free yet serious lasagna-inspired pasta, my noodle of choice is campanelle. It's shaped like an adorable flower, is reminiscent of a lasagna noodle with its curvy edges, and scoops up the cheesy meat sauce perfectly. But you can also totally use ziti (same cook time). This dish has all of the flavors of lasagna with none of the mess!

Prep Time	Sauté Time	Pressure Building Time	Pressure Cook Time	Total Time	Serves
5 minutes	**10** minutes	**10–15** minutes	**6** minutes	**35** minutes	**4–6**

THE PASTA

1   tablespoon extra-virgin olive oil

1   yellow onion, diced

3   cloves garlic, minced or pressed

1½ pounds ground beef or meatloaf mixture

4   cups Marinara Sauce (page 34; but look for the Victoria brand if you don't feel like making your own)

3   cups garlic broth (e.g. Garlic Better Than Bouillon) or beef broth

1–2 tablespoons hot sauce (optional)

1   pound campanelle

THE LASAGNA CHEESE

1   cup ricotta cheese

1   large egg

1   teaspoon dried parsley flakes

½   teaspoon kosher salt

1   (5.2-ounce) package Boursin spread (any flavor) or 4 ounces cream cheese, cut into chunky cubes

2   cups shredded mozzarella cheese

⅓   cup grated Parmesan cheese

1 Pour the olive oil into the Instant Pot and then hit Sauté and Adjust so it's on the More or High setting. Heat the oil for 3 minutes.

2 Add the onion and cook for 2 minutes, until lightly softened and translucent. Add the garlic and cook for another minute.

3 Add the ground beef and cook, stirring constantly to crumble, until lightly browned (about 2 minutes), scraping up any browned bits from the bottom of the pot.

CONTINUES

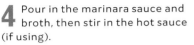

4 Pour in the marinara sauce and broth, then stir in the hot sauce (if using).

5 Add the campanelle but *do not stir*—just smooth it out with a spoon so it's submerged in the sauce. It's okay if a few bits stick out above the surface.

6 Secure the lid, move the valve to the sealing position, hit Keep Warm/Cancel, and then hit Manual or Pressure Cook on High Pressure for 6 minutes. Quick release when done.

7 Meanwhile, combine the ricotta, egg, dried parsley, and salt in a mixing bowl.

8 When the pot's done, stir in the ricotta mixture (don't worry—the raw egg will quickly be cooked by the heat from the pot's contents), Boursin or cream cheese, mozzarella, and Parmesan.

9 Serve topped with extra Parmesan, if desired.

JEFF'S TIPS

For a golden cheese top, you have two choices:

1. If using the Instant Pot Duo Crisp, add an additional 1–2 cups of shredded mozzarella cheese. Then, add the crisping lid and hit Bake at 400°F for 3–5 minutes or until the cheese is melted and browned to your desired consistency and color.

2. Simply transfer the finished pasta to a casserole dish, cover with another 1–2 cups of shredded mozzarella, and pop it in a preheated oven at 400°F, uncovered, for 5–10 minutes, until the cheese lightly bubbles and browns (be sure to keep an eye on it, as oven temperatures vary).

BUTTER CHICKEN BOWTIES

Oh, you know me. Always marrying two different cuisines and acting crazy. This time, it's a classic Indian butter chicken falling in love with bowtie pasta. And it's a good thing because this dish is so grand, it's a bowtie affair.

Prep Time	Sauté Time	Pressure Building Time	Pressure Cook Time	Total Time	Serves
5 minutes	**10** minutes	**5–10** minutes	**6** minutes	**30** minutes	**4–6**

- **8 tablespoons (1 stick) salted butter**
- **1 medium yellow onion, diced**
- **3 cloves garlic, minced or pressed**
- **2 pounds boneless, skinless chicken thighs or breasts, cut into bite-size chunks**
- **2 tablespoons garam masala powder, divided in half (see Jeff's Tips)**

- **2 teaspoons curry powder**
- **1 teaspoon ground ginger powder**
- **1 teaspoon ground cumin**
- **2 cups chicken or garlic broth (e.g. Garlic Better Than Bouillon)**
- **1 (14-ounce) can unsweetened coconut milk (it should be thin like water and not thick and lumpy)**

- **1 pound farfalle (bowtie) pasta**
- **1 (6-ounce) can tomato paste**
- **¼ cup heavy cream or half-and-half**
- **1 teaspoon seasoned salt**

TO SERVE (OPTIONAL)
Fresh cilantro
Crumbled paneer (Indian cheese) or feta cheese

1 On the Instant Pot, hit Sauté and Adjust so it's on the More or High setting. Put in the butter and, once melted, add the onion and sauté for 2–3 minutes until lightly translucent. Add the garlic and sauté for 1 minute longer.

2 Add the chicken and sear while stirring constantly for 2 minutes until the sides become pinkish-white in color (but not fully cooked yet). Add 1 tablespoon of the garam masala along with the curry powder, ginger powder, and cumin and stir for 1 minute more.

CONTINUES

3 Pour in the chicken broth and the coconut milk and stir until combined. Add the farfalle but *do not stir!* Simply smooth it out so it's lightly submerged in the liquid. It is perfectly fine for the pasta to be a little above the liquid.

4 Secure the lid, move the valve to the sealing position, hit Keep Warm/Cancel and then hit Manual or Pressure Cook on High Pressure for 6 minutes. Quick release when done.

5 Stir in the tomato paste, cream, the remaining tablespoon of garam masala, and the seasoned salt.

6 Serve topped with fresh cilantro and crumbled paneer or feta, if desired.

JEFF'S TIPS

Garam masala is crucial to achieve that signature butter chicken flavor. You can find it at most markets with a broad spice section, at an international market, or online.

Want it creamier? Add up to ½ cup of cream, Greek yogurt, or cashew or almond milk.

This dish is only mildly spicy, if at all. If you want it spicier, feel free to add a little cayenne pepper in Step 5. I would start with ⅛ teaspoon and adjust from there, as a little goes a long way.

ROTINI RANCHERO

Here's a totally new way to do Taco Tuesday. This is a smooth tomato-and-cheese pasta packed with taco-seasoned ground beef in a ranchero-style sauce. This recipe is a hit not only with adults, but kids can't get enough of it either.

Prep Time	Sauté Time	Pressure Building Time	Pressure Cook Time	Total Time	Serves
5 minutes	10 minutes	5–10 minutes	5 minutes	30 minutes	4–6

2 tablespoons extra-virgin olive oil

1 medium yellow onion, diced

1 pound ground beef or ground turkey

3 cups beef broth

16 ounces red salsa of your choice

1 packet taco seasoning

1 pound rotini

2 cups shredded Mexican cheese blend, plus more for topping

½ cup crumbled cotija cheese

1 (8-ounce) can diced green chilies

10 ounces frozen corn (optional)

TO SERVE (OPTIONAL)
Sliced jalapeños
Black olives, pitted and sliced

1 On the Instant Pot, hit Sauté and Adjust so it's on the More or High setting. Pour in the olive oil and heat for about 3 minutes, then add the onion and sauté for 2–3 minutes, until softened. Add the ground beef and sauté, stirring constantly, for 2–3 minutes, until lightly browned.

2 Add the broth, salsa, and taco seasoning and stir well. Add the pasta but *do not stir*—just use a spoon to submerge it under the liquid. It is okay if some pokes out above the surface.

3 Secure the lid, move the valve to the sealing position, and hit Keep Warm/Cancel and then hit Manual or Pressure Cook on High Pressure for 5 minutes. Quick release when done.

JEFF'S TIPS

If you can't find cotija cheese, you can use grated Parmesan instead.

If you wish to give it a cheesy, melty top, follow the suggestions in my Lasagna Bouquets (page 98).

4 Stir in the cheeses and green chilies. Then, add in the corn (if using) until well combined and the corn is heated through (which will be within a matter of minutes due to the heat of the pasta.)

5 Serve with sliced jalapeños, black olives, more cheese, or your favorite taco toppings.

TUSCAN TORTELLINI

I love any creamy mushroom pasta, but this one takes it to the next level. We're talking a trip to Tuscany in one bite.

Prep Time	Sauté Time	Pressure Building Time	Pressure Cook Time	Total Time	Serves
5 minutes	**10** minutes	**5–10** minutes	**0–2** minutes	**25** minutes	**4–6**

4   tablespoons (½ stick) salted butter

1   large shallot, diced

1   pound baby bella mushrooms, sliced

6   cloves garlic, minced or pressed

3   cups mushroom broth (e.g. Mushroom Better Than Bouillon) or chicken broth

½   teaspoon black pepper

⅛   teaspoon ground nutmeg

24 ounces fresh tortellini of your choice

5   ounces baby spinach

5   ounces frozen peas

¾   cup grated Parmesan cheese

½   cup heavy cream or half-and-half

¼   cup pesto sauce (optional; Costco has the best)

1   (5.2-ounce) package Boursin spread (any flavor) or 4 ounces cream cheese, cut into chunky cubes

Truffle oil, for serving (optional)

1 On the Instant Pot, hit Sauté and Adjust so it's on the More or High setting. Put in the butter and wait until it melts. Add the shallot and mushrooms and sauté, stirring, for about 3 minutes. Add the garlic and sauté for 1 minute longer.

2 Add the broth, pepper, and nutmeg and stir well. Add the tortellini and use a wooden spoon to gently submerge it in the broth, but *do not stir*. Top off with the spinach but, again, *do not stir*. (It's going to feel like there's a *lot* of spinach in there and it will come up to the brim of the pot, but don't worry—it cooks down to nothing!)

3 Secure the lid, move the valve to the sealing position, and hit Keep Warm/Cancel, then Manual or Pressure Cook on High Pressure for 0 minutes for slightly firmer pasta and 2 minutes for softer. When done, use a quick release.

4 Remove the lid, hit Keep Warm/Cancel and then Sauté and Adjust so it's on the More or High setting, then add the frozen peas (no need to defrost beforehand) and stir to combine.

5 Add the Parmesan, heavy cream, pesto (if using), and Boursin or cream cheese. Cook, stirring occasionally, until completely melted (2–3 minutes). Hit Keep Warm/Cancel and let sit for a few minutes, until thickened.

6 Serve drizzled with truffle oil, if desired.

 JEFF'S TIPS You can usually find fresh tortellini in the refrigerated section of your local supermarket.

If using frozen tortellini, go for 5 minutes of pressure cooking time.

Feel like fresh or frozen ravioli instead? No problem! Just add 2 minutes of pressure cooking time for fresh ravioli and 7 minutes for frozen.

RICE

One of the best things about the Instant Pot is how versatile it is. It can make roasts, soups, desserts—and even replace your rice cooker. Here, I'll share some of my favorite rice dishes with you, both classic and totally new.

Hibachi Fried Rice 108	**Butternut Squash Risotto** 114	**Tex-Mex Brown Rice & Beans** 120
Arroz con Pollo 110	**Lemon Asparagus Parmesan Risotto** 116	**Sticky Nashville Hot Chicken & Rice** 122
Mushroom Risotto 112	**Jambalaya** 118	**Thai Basil Fried Rice** 124

HIBACHI FRIED RICE

Every time I go out for hibachi, there's just one thing I crave: that simple yet packed-full-of-flavor fried rice—with the amazing sauces to go with it. It's the thing I look forward to the most (minus the part where I come home smelling like a hibachi sauna). And now you can make it yourself, at home, in your Instant Pot—with no scent to follow you anywhere.

Prep Time	Sauté Time	Pressure Building Time	Pressure Cook Time	Natural Release Time	Total Time	Serves
5 minutes	5–10 minutes	5–10 minutes	3 minutes	10 Minutes	35 minutes	4–6

- 2 cups jasmine rice
- 2 cups water
- 2 tablespoons sesame oil
- 1 large white or yellow onion, diced
- 1 (10-ounce) box frozen peas and carrots mix
- 1 (10-ounce) box frozen sweet kernel corn
- 1 tablespoon salted butter
- 3 large eggs
- 3 tablespoons low-sodium soy sauce
- Sesame seeds

1 In a strainer, rinse the rice thoroughly until the water draining from it runs clear, about 90 seconds.

2 Place the rinsed and drained rice in the Instant Pot along with the water and stir.

3 Secure the lid, move the valve to the sealing position, and hit Manual or Pressure Cook on High Pressure for 3 minutes. When done, use a natural release for 10 minutes followed by a quick release. Fluff the rice with a fork, transfer to a serving bowl, and set aside.

4 On the Instant Pot (no need to clean the liner pot first), hit Keep Warm/Cancel, pour in the sesame oil, and hit Sauté and Adjust so it's on the More or High setting

5 Once the oil begins to sizzle, scrape up the browned bits of rice from the bottom of the pan with a wooden spoon and add the onion. Let cook for about a minute and then add the peas and carrots mix and corn. Add the butter and cook, stirring, for 3 minutes.

6 Move the veggies to one side of the pot. Crack the eggs into the other side and stir constantly to scramble and cook. Once the egg has just cooked through, mix it in with the veggies for a few moments until fully cooked.

7 Hit Keep Warm/Cancel and return the rice to the pot. Add in the soy sauce, shake in a generous amount of sesame seeds, and mix everything together before serving.

 JEFF'S TIP For a great finishing touch, make any of the following sauces and use to top individual bowls of rice.

JAPANESE MUSTARD SAUCE

¼ cup soy sauce

¼ cup milk

2 tablespoons heavy cream

2 tablespoons ground mustard powder

1½ teaspoons sugar

1 clove garlic, minced or pressed

JAPANESE GINGER SAUCE

½ cup soy sauce

2 tablespoons minced ginger

Juice of ½ lemon

1 clove garlic, minced

1½ teaspoons onion powder

½ teaspoon sugar

¼ teaspoon white vinegar

JAPANESE MAYO SAUCE

1 cup mayonnaise

2 tablespoons water

1 tablespoon melted unsalted butter

1 teaspoon tomato paste

1 teaspoon sugar

½ teaspoon paprika

½ teaspoon garlic powder

½ teaspoon salt

ARROZ CON POLLO

Arroz con pollo means "rice with chicken" and is a staple at many Spanish restaurants. I can't resist ordering it whenever I see it on a menu—and all the scrumptious variations I've tried led me to this recipe. What sets it apart is the addition of chorizo, a classic Spanish sausage.

Prep Time	Sauté Time	Pressure Building Time	Pressure Cook Time	Total Time	Serves
10 minutes	10 minutes	10–15 minutes	10 minutes	45 minutes	4–6

- 2 tablespoons extra-virgin olive oil
- 2 tablespoons (¼ stick) salted butter
- ½ teaspoon (a generous pinch) saffron
- 1 medium yellow onion, diced
- 1 red bell pepper, diced
- 3 cloves garlic, minced

- 2 pounds boneless, skinless chicken thighs, cut into bite-size pieces
- 1 pound chorizo, sliced into ¼-inch disks (if your market sells only crumbled, loose chorizo, that's fine too)
- 2 teaspoons paprika
- 2 teaspoons ground cumin
- 2 teaspoons dried parsley

- 1 teaspoon chili powder
- 1 cup dry white wine (like a sauvignon blanc)
- 3 cups chicken broth
- Juice of 1 lime
- 1 (14.5-ounce) can diced tomatoes, with their juices
- 14 ounces Goya arroz amarillo or other yellow rice

1 Place the oil and butter in the Instant Pot and hit Sauté and Adjust so it's on the More or High setting. Once the butter's melted, add the saffron and sauté for 30 seconds, until fragrant.

2 Add the onion and bell pepper and sauté, stirring, for 3 minutes, until they begin to soften. Add the garlic and sauté for another minute.

3 Add the chicken and chorizo and stir to coat, followed by the paprika, cumin, parsley flakes, and chili powder. Sauté, stirring constantly so the spices don't stick to the bottom of the pot, for 3 minutes, until the chicken is no longer pink on the outside.

JEFF'S TIP Saffron is pricey compared to most spices, but it lasts forever and a little goes a long way. I think it's key for this dish, but if you don't wish to use it, it's not the end of the world.

4 Add the white wine and allow everything to simmer in it for 1 minute. Add the broth, lime juice, and diced tomatoes with their juices. Stir well and bring to a simmer.

5 Once it's bubbling, add the rice but *do not stir* it in—just use a mixing spoon to lightly submerge it under the broth.

6 Secure the lid, move the valve to the sealing position, hit Keep Warm/Cancel and then hit Manual or Pressure Cook on High Pressure for 10 minutes. Quick release when done.

7 Don't worry if it looks like there's too much liquid—just stir everything together and the excess liquid will become a lush and velvety sauce. Let stand for about 5 minutes, until the sauce has thickened to your liking.

8 Serve and enjoy with my Refried Beans (page 242).

MUSHROOM RISOTTO

Do you believe in magic? You're going to once you see how the Instant Pot changes your risotto game. This supreme dish requires zero babysitting but is still cooked to rich and creamy, shroomy perfection.

Prep Time	Sauté Time	Pressure Building Time	Pressure Cook Time	Total Time	Serves
5 minutes	**10** minutes	**5–10** minutes	**6** minutes	**30** minutes	**4–6**

- **1 tablespoon vegetable oil**
- **4 tablespoons (½ stick) salted butter**
- **2 large shallots, minced**
- **3 cloves garlic, minced or pressed**

- **1½ pounds baby bella mushrooms, sliced**
- **½ cup dry white wine (like a chardonnay)**
- **2 cups arborio rice**
- **4½ cups mushroom broth (e.g. Mushroom Better Than Bouillon) or chicken broth**

- **1 teaspoon seasoned salt**
- **½ teaspoon black pepper**
- **½ teaspoon Italian seasoning**
- **½ cup grated Parmesan cheese**
- **1 tablespoon white or black truffle oil**

1 Place the vegetable oil and butter in the Instant Pot. Hit Sauté and Adjust so it's on the More or High setting and heat until the butter has just begun to bubble.

2 Add the shallots and cook for about 2 minutes, until softened. Then add the garlic and sauté for 1 minute longer.

3 Add the mushrooms and cook, stirring constantly, until the mushrooms have browned and cooked down a bit, about 2 minutes.

JEFF'S TIP You know I love to let you make my recipes your own, but here's my one rule: when you make risotto (any risotto), you absolutely must use arborio rice. Other rices won't get creamy and you'll end up with a gloppy mess.

4 Add the white wine and bring to a simmer for 3 minutes, stirring and scraping up any browned bits from the bottom of the pot.

5 Stir in the rice and sauté for 1 minute.

6 Add the broth, seasoned salt, black pepper, and Italian seasoning. Stir well, giving the bottom of the pot a few last good scrapes so nothing's stuck on.

7 Secure the lid, move the valve to the sealing position, hit Keep Warm/Cancel and then Manual or Pressure Cook on High Pressure for 6 minutes. Quick release when done.

8 Add the grated Parmesan and truffle oil, stir well until combined, and serve.

BUTTERNUT SQUASH
RISOTTO

Risotto is the pasta of the rice world, and this is the first thing to go from any table I put it down on. At my family Thanksgiving, this dish is so popular, Tom Turkey might pray it shows up so all eyes are on this instead of him.

Prep Time	Sauté Time	Pressure Building Time	Pressure Cook Time	Total Time	Serves
5 minutes	**10** minutes	**5–10** minutes	**6** minutes	**30** minutes	**4–6**

1 **tablespoon vegetable oil**

2 **tablespoons (¼ stick) salted butter**

1 **medium yellow onion, diced**

4 **cups butternut squash (from about 1 medium-size squash), peeled and cut into 1-inch pieces, any seeds and stringy insides removed**

3 **cloves garlic, minced or pressed**

½ **cup dry white wine (like a chardonnay)**

2 **cups arborio rice**

4½ **cups turkey broth (e.g. Turkey Better Than Bouillon) or chicken or vegetable broth**

1 **teaspoon seasoned salt**

½ **teaspoon white pepper**

½ **teaspoon Italian seasoning**

¼ **teaspoon nutmeg**

5–8 **ounces baby spinach**

½ **cup grated Parmesan cheese**

1 Place the oil and butter in the Instant Pot. Hit Sauté and Adjust so it's on the More or High setting and heat until the butter begins to bubble.

2 Add the onion and cook for about 2 minutes, until softened. Add the butternut squash and stir for another 1–2 minutes (the squash will be hard, but don't worry—it will completely soften up after pressure cooking). Add the garlic and sauté, stirring, for another 3 minutes, until the onion is slightly translucent and everything smells delicious.

3 Add the white wine, bring to a simmer, and simmer for another 2 minutes before adding the rice.

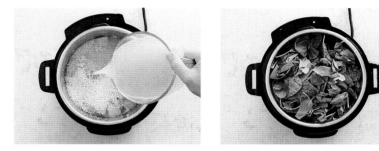 

4 Add the broth, seasoned salt, white pepper, Italian seasoning, and nutmeg and stir well, scraping up any browned bits from the bottom of the pot. Place the spinach on top, but *do not mix it in*—just let it rest on top. It may look like a lot of spinach, but you'll be shocked at how it cooks down to nothing.

5 Secure the lid, turn the valve to the sealing position, and hit Manual or Pressure Cook on High Pressure for 6 minutes. Quick release when done, add the grated Parmesan, and stir everything together before serving.

JEFF'S TIP Many markets and wholesale clubs sell butternut squash precut into cubes, which I prefer to use as they save so much time and hassle—about 24 ounces should be enough.

LEMON ASPARAGUS
PARMESAN
RISOTTO

When your creamy risotto incorporates a lemon Parmesan sauce tossed with sweet asparagus, life just got better.

Prep Time	Sauté Time	Pressure Building Time	Pressure Cook Time	Total Time	Serves
5 minutes	**7** minutes	**10–15** minutes	**6** minutes	**30** minutes	**4–6**

1 tablespoon vegetable oil

4 tablespoons (½ stick) salted butter

2 large shallots, diced

1 pound asparagus, tough bottom ends discarded, tips separated and the rest of the stalks cut into bite-size pieces

3 cloves garlic, minced or pressed

½ cup dry white wine (like a chardonnay)

Juice of 2 lemons (plus the zest for serving; optional)

2 cups arborio rice

4½ cups chicken or vegetable broth

1 teaspoon seasoned salt

½ teaspoon black pepper

½ teaspoon Italian seasoning

1 cup grated Parmesan cheese, plus more for topping

¼ cup heavy cream or half-and-half

1 Hit Sauté and Adjust so the pot is on the More or High setting. Place the oil and butter in the pot and cook until just beginning to bubble.

2 Add the shallots and cook for about 2 minutes, until softened. Add the asparagus stalks (not the tips) and garlic and sauté for another 2 minutes.

3 Add the wine and lemon juice and bring to a simmer, scraping up any browned bits from the bottom of the pot. Add the rice and sauté, stirring, for 1 minute.

4 Add the broth, seasoned salt, black pepper, and Italian seasoning. Stir well, again scraping the bottom of the pot to make sure nothing's stuck.

5 Secure the lid, turn the valve to the sealing position, and hit Keep Warm/Cancel then Manual or Pressure Cook on High Pressure for 6 minutes. Quick release when done.

6 As the risotto's cooking, place the asparagus tips and 1 tablespoon water in a microwave-safe bowl, cover with plastic wrap, and microwave for 1 minute. Keep the cover on and set aside until the next step.

7 When the lid is off, stir in the steamed asparagus tips, the grated Parmesan cheese, and the heavy cream and let stand until thickened, about 2 minutes. Serve topped with more Parmesan and/or lemon zest, if desired.

JEFF'S TIPS

Serve this with crusty garlic bread. It's nirvana.

If you don't feel like microwaving the asparagus tips and don't mind them softer, you can add them to the pot along with the asparagus stalks before pressure cooking.

JAMBALAYA

There's no one way to make jambalaya, a classic New Orleans rice dish with seafood and sausage. And people will always swear by their own versions of it. But trust me: my spin on this classic dish could conjure a brass band parade strutting through your kitchen.

Prep Time	Sauté Time	Pressure Building Time	Pressure Cook Time	Total Time	Serves
10 minutes	**15** minutes	**10–15** minutes	**10** minutes	**50** minutes	**4–6**

4 tablespoons (½ stick) salted butter

24 ounces andouille or any precooked smoked sausage, sliced ½ inch thick

2 tablespoons paprika

1 tablespoon cumin

1 teaspoon seasoned salt

1 teaspoon light- or dark-brown sugar

½ teaspoon Cajun or Creole seasoning

½ teaspoon black pepper

½ teaspoon cayenne pepper (optional)

1 (14.5-ounce) can diced tomatoes, with their juices

2 large green bell peppers, diced

2 ribs celery, sliced ¼ inch thick

1 bunch scallions, thinly sliced

1 cup dry red wine (like a cabernet)

3 cups chicken broth

14 ounces Goya arroz amarillo (yellow rice)

1½ pounds large shrimp, peeled and deveined

JEFF'S TIPS Can't find yellow rice? Use any long-grain white rice instead, but use a 5-minute natural release followed by a quick release when done.

While pressure cooking, the timer may begin to count down on the display **BEFORE** the pressure pin pops up. If this happens, it's fine. It will eventually push up—and if it doesn't, the dish will still come out great as intended! Sometimes having a lot going on in the pot can confuse the calibration.

1 Place the butter in the Instant Pot and hit Sauté and Adjust until it's on the High or More setting. Once the butter's melted, add the sausage and cook for 2 minutes, until lightly browned.

2 Add the paprika, cumin, seasoned salt, brown sugar, Cajun or Creole seasoning, black pepper, and cayenne (if using). Sauté, stirring, for 1 minute, then add the canned tomatoes with their juices and stir well.

3 Add the bell peppers, celery, and scallions and cook, stirring constantly, for 3 minutes. Add the wine and broth and bring to a bubble. Add the rice but *do not stir it in*—just use a mixing spoon to lightly submerge it in the liquid.

4 Secure the lid, move the valve to the sealing position, hit Keep Warm/Cancel and then Manual or Pressure Cook on High Pressure for 10 minutes. Quick release when done. When you remove the lid, don't worry if the dish looks too soupy! It will thicken up as soon as you give it a stir.

5 Press the Keep Warm/Cancel button and hit Sauté and Adjust so it's on Normal or Medium. Add the shrimp and cook, stirring often and scraping the bottom of the pot to ensure the rice does not stick, for 5–6 minutes, until the shrimp are curled and opaque and the jambalaya has thickened. Then hit Keep Warm/Cancel or just Keep Warm until ready to serve.

TEX-MEX
BROWN RICE & BEANS

Sometimes the simplest dishes are the tastiest. Making it healthier with brown rice is perfect for an impromptu burrito bowl night. Just top with shredded cheese, lettuce, chopped tomatoes, or anything else your family loves.

Prep Time	Pressure Building Time	Pressure Cook Time	Natural Release Time	Total Time	Serves
5 minutes	**10–15** minutes	**25** minutes	**10** minutes	**55** minutes	**4**

2 cups brown rice, rinsed
3 cups vegetable broth or chicken broth
1 cup salsa (use your favorite)
3 teaspoons ground cumin

2 teaspoons Goya sazón seasoning (any flavor you choose)
1 (15.5-ounce) can black beans or red kidney beans, drained and rinsed

1½ teaspoons seasoned salt
    Juice of ½ lime (optional)

TO SERVE (OPTIONAL)
Chopped cilantro
Shredded Mexican cheese blend

1 Using a fine-mesh strainer, rinse the rice until the water draining from it runs clear. Place the drained rice in the Instant Pot along with the broth, salsa, cumin, sazón, and beans. Stir well.

2 Secure the lid, turn the valve to the sealing position, and hit Manual or Pressure Cook on High Pressure for 25 minutes. Allow a 10-minute natural release and then finish with a quick release.

3 Give it a stir and add the seasoned salt and lime juice (if using), then stir again until combined.

4 Top with fresh cilantro and shredded cheese, if desired, and serve.

 JEFF'S TIP This recipe will work great with any rice or grain of your choice—just make sure you adjust the liquid ratio according to the chart on page 38.

STICKY
NASHVILLE
HOT CHICKEN
& RICE

Oooo-EEEE! Nashville hot chicken takes classic fried chicken and amps the spice up to 11. Since the Instant Pot can't deep-fry, I created this seared chicken-and-rice dish with a sauce inspired by its unmistakable spiciness. If you're not a fan of the extreme heat, feel free to take it easy on the spices—it'll still be delicious.

Prep Time	Sauté Time	Pressure Building Time	Pressure Cook Time	Natural Release Time	Total Time	Serves
10 minutes	6 minutes	5–10 minutes	3 minutes	10 minutes	40 minutes	4–6

THE CHICKEN & RICE

- **2** tablespoons vegetable oil
- **2** tablespoons (¼ stick) salted butter
- **1** Vidalia (sweet) onion, diced
- **2** pounds boneless, skinless chicken thighs, cut into bite-size pieces
- **6** cloves garlic, minced or pressed
- **2** cups chicken broth, divided
- **2** cups jasmine rice, rinsed and drained
- **1** bunch scallions, thinly sliced

THE NASHVILLE HOT SAUCE

- **⅔** cup hot sauce (I use Frank's RedHot)
- **⅓** cup vegetable oil
- **1** tablespoon brown sugar
- **1** tablespoon cayenne pepper
- **2** teaspoons paprika
- **1** teaspoon chili powder
- **1** teaspoon garlic powder

1 On the Instant Pot, hit Sauté and Adjust so it's on More or High. Place the oil and butter in the pot. Once the butter has melted, add the onion and sauté until softened and just beginning to brown, 2–3 minutes.

2 Add the chicken and garlic and sauté for another 2–3 minutes, until the chicken has just begun to turn pinkish-white around the edges.

3 Pour in ½ cup of the broth and scrape up the browned bits from the bottom of the pot with a wooden spoon. Add the rice and the remaining broth and stir.

5 Meanwhile, make the Nashville Hot Sauce by whisking together all the ingredients.

4 Secure the lid, turn the valve to the sealing position, hit Keep Warm/Cancel and then Manual or Pressure Cook on High Pressure for 3 minutes. When done, allow a 10-minute natural release and finish with a quick release.

6 When the pot's done, fluff the rice with a fork, add in the sauce, and mix well until the chicken and rice are coated. Top with scallions and serve.

JEFF'S TIPS

WARNING: This is one *spicy* dish! If you don't like it so hot, start with only ⅛ teaspoon of cayenne pepper and add more at the end if the spirit moves you.

Not all hot sauces are created equal! Whichever you choose, be sure to remember that the hotter the sauce, the more intense the experience.

THAI BASIL FRIED RICE

This is one of my longtime favorite comfort dishes—spicy, sweet fried rice tossed in just the right amount of joy. The best part is, you don't even need to find Thai basil to make it. Tarragon will do just perfectly.

Prep Time	Sauté Time	Pressure Building Time	Pressure Cook Time	Natural Release Time	Total Time	Serves
5 minutes	10–12 minutes	5–10 minutes	3 minutes	10 minutes	40 minutes	4–6

2 cups jasmine rice

2 cups water or garlic broth (e.g. Garlic Better Than Bouillon)

½ cup vegetable oil

1 large Vidalia (sweet) onion, diced

1 large red bell pepper, diced

2 jalapeño peppers, diced (for some heat; optional)

2 cups Thai basil leaves *or* fresh tarragon leaves (I use this and it works like a charm), reserving a few for garnish

9 cloves garlic, minced or pressed

3 large eggs

1 pound shrimp, tails on or off, deveined and peeled (optional)

¼ cup low-sodium soy sauce

¼ cup oyster sauce

2 tablespoons fish sauce

2 tablespoons pad thai sauce

1 In a fine-mesh strainer, rinse the rice thoroughly, until the water draining from it runs clear, about 90 seconds. Place the rinsed and drained rice in the Instant Pot along with the water or broth and stir.

2 Secure the lid, move the valve to the sealing position, hit Keep Warm/Cancel and then hit Manual or Pressure Cook on High Pressure for 3 minutes. When done, allow a 10-minute natural release followed by a quick release.

3 Fluff the rice with a fork, transfer to a bowl, and let rest.

4 On the Instant Pot (no need to clean the liner pot first), hit Sauté and Adjust so it's on the More or High setting. Add the oil, and once it's heated, add in the onion, bell pepper, jalapeño (if using), and Thai basil or tarragon leaves and sauté for 5 minutes, until slightly softened. Add in the garlic and cook for 1 minute longer.

5 Move the veggies to one side of the pot. Crack the eggs into the other side and stir constantly to scramble and cook. Once the eggs have just cooked through, mix them in with the veggies for a few moments, until fully cooked.

6 Add in the shrimp (if using), and cook them until they are curled and opaque, 3–5 minutes. Hit Keep Warm/Cancel to turn the pot off.

7 Add the rice back to the pot and top with the soy sauce, oyster sauce, fish sauce, and pad thai sauce. Stir until it fully combines into the rice. Garnish with the reserved Thai basil or tarragon and serve.

 JEFF'S TIP **Want to sub in chicken for the shrimp? I gotcha!** Add in 1 pound of diced chicken breasts while you add the egg in Step 5 and sauté until fully cooked.

5

POULTRY

Every Instant Pot fanatic knows that
"Winner, winner! Chicken dinner!" may be the motto of the Instant
Pot. Every chicken dish I've ever created for this device
has been juicy, mouthwatering, and memorable—with no fussy
cleanup and no babysitting a pan on the stove. These delicious
dishes will become your new weeknight wins.

French Onion
Chicken
128

Chicken &
Dumplings
131

Chicken Marsala
135

Mall Food Court
Bourbon Chicken
138

Chicken &
Broccoli
140

Chicken
Shawarma
142

White Queso
Chicken
Enchilada
Casserole
144

Turkey Breast
& Gravy
147

Creamy Curry
Chicken
150

Chicken
Scarpariello
152

Tangy Chicken
Wings
154

Chicken à la
Queens
156

Chicken
Oreganata
159

Ménage à Thai
Chicken Curry
(Curry Three
Ways)
161

Fiesta Chicken
Tacos
164

Chicken Feta
Florentine
166

Buffalo Chicken
Wraps
168

FRENCH ONION CHICKEN

My favorite soup of all time is deep, rich French onion. And one day, as I was slurping a bowl, a magical thought occurred to me: I could turn the broth into a sauce to be draped over chicken lying on a bed of garlic toast, tucked in with a blanket of melted cheese. And the rest, my friends, is history. French Onion Chicken, a star in its own right, was born. You can usually find Texas toast or garlic bread in the freezer section of your market.

Prep Time	Sauté Time	Pressure Building Time	Pressure Cook Time	Optional Oven Time	Total Time	Serves
5 minutes	**20** minutes	**5–10** minutes	**5** minutes	**5** minutes	**45** minutes	**4–6**

- **2 pounds boneless, skinless chicken breasts, each breast sliced crosswise into fillets about ¼ inch thick**
- **½ cup all-purpose flour (with a few pinches of onion powder, garlic salt, and black pepper mixed in) for dredging**
- **¼ cup extra-virgin olive oil**

- **4 tablespoons (½ stick) salted butter, divided**
- **2 Vidalia (sweet) onions, sliced into strands**
- **2 (18.5-ounce) cans non-condensed French onion soup**

- **6–8 slices Texas toast (any variety) or frozen garlic bread**
- **3 tablespoons cornstarch**
- **1 packet onion soup/dip mix (optional)**
- **8–10 Swiss cheese slices**
- **Crispy fried onions, for serving (optional)**

1 Coat the chicken in the flour mixture and set aside.

2 Place the olive oil and 2 tablespoons of the butter in the Instant Pot, hit Sauté and Adjust to the High or More setting, and allow to heat for 3 minutes, until the butter's melted.

3 Working in batches, sear the chicken for 1 minute on each side until very lightly browned, remove the chicken with tongs, and set aside on a plate. Leave any excess oil in the pot for more flavor.

CONTINUES

JEFF'S TIP

You may ask: "We already use a few cans of French onion soup and a packet of onion soup mix—why do I need to add *more* onions?" You don't *need* to—but I highly recommend it. The onions in the canned soup and soup mix don't have a lot of body and texture, so the fresh and crispy onions give you a little something to bite into.

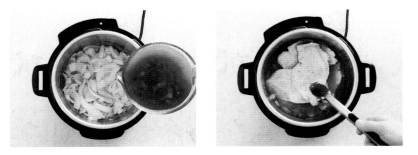

4 Add the remaining 2 tablespoons of butter to the pot and, once melted, add the onions. Sauté for about 10 minutes until they soften and become a bit browned (but not burned), stirring and scraping up any browned bits from the bottom of the pot.

5 Add the canned onion soup and stir. Return the chicken to the pot.

6 Secure the lid, move the valve to the sealing position, hit Keep Warm/ Cancel, and then hit Manual or Pressure Cook on High Pressure for 5 minutes. Quick release when done.

7 While the chicken is cooking, make the Texas toast (or garlic bread) according to package instructions. When done, line a casserole dish with the toast.

8 When the lid comes off the pot, remove the chicken with tongs and set aside (but leave the sauce in the pot). Hit Keep Warm/Cancel and then hit Sauté again so it's on More or High.

9 Make the cornstarch slurry by mixing the cornstarch with 3 tablespoons of water. Add the slurry to the pot along with the onion soup mix (if using) and stir until well combined. Bring to a bubble and cook for about 1 minute, stirring constantly, and then turn off the pot. Let the sauce sit for a few moments until thickened.

10 Layer the chicken over the bread, cover with some of the sauce, place a slice of cheese over it, and add a little more sauce to top it all off. You can pop it into the oven to broil for about 5 minutes so it bubbles and browns (which I recommend). Sprinkle with some crispy fried onions if you're feeling onion crazy!

CHICKEN & DUMPLINGS

This creamy Southern classic has many interpretations—the "dumplings" in particular. In my popular version, I cut my dumplings into ribbons—almost like homemade noodles for this home-style chicken stew. This easy recipe has you getting just a little fancy—and it's going to taste even fancier.

Prep Time	Sauté Time	Pressure Building Time	Pressure Cook Time	Total Time	Serves
15 minutes	**20** minutes	**10–15** minutes	**10** minutes	**60** minutes	**4–6**

THE CHICKEN

- **4** tablespoons (½ stick) salted butter
- **1** yellow onion, diced
- **2** large carrots, peeled and diced
- **3** ribs celery, sliced into ¼-inch pieces, leafy tops reserved
- **3** cloves garlic, minced or pressed
- **6** cups chicken broth
- **1** whole chicken (4–5 pounds), chopped into quarters (leg, breast, thigh, and wing; your market's butcher will usually do this for you if you ask nicely)
- **3** bay leaves
- **½** cup cooking sherry
- **1½** teaspoons seasoned salt
- **1½** teaspoons poultry seasoning
- **1½** teaspoons black pepper
- **1½** teaspoons dried sage
- **1** teaspoon dried thyme

THE DUMPLINGS

- **1¼** cups all-purpose flour, plus more for dusting
- **2** teaspoons baking powder
- **1** teaspoon salt
- **½** cup whole milk
- **2** tablespoons (¼ stick) salted butter
- **3** tablespoons cornstarch
- **½** cup heavy cream or half-and-half

MAKE THE CHICKEN

1 Place the butter in the Instant Pot and hit Sauté and Adjust so it's on the More or High setting. Once melted, add the onion, carrots, and celery and sauté for 5 minutes, until everything is softened. Add the garlic and sauté for 1 minute longer.

2 Pour in the broth and stir well. Add the chicken and make sure it's all covered by the broth. Toss in the bay leaves.

3 Secure the lid, move the valve to the sealing position, hit Keep Warm/Cancel, and then hit Manual or Pressure Cook on High Pressure for 10 minutes. Quick release when done.

CONTINUES

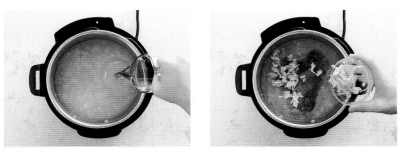

4 Use tongs to remove the chicken from the pot and set aside. Discard the bay leaves.

5 Add the cooking sherry, seasoned salt, poultry seasoning, pepper, sage, thyme, and leafy tops from the celery to the pot and stir well.

MAKE THE DUMPLINGS

6 In a mixing bowl, whisk together the flour, baking powder, and salt.

7 Place the milk and butter in a Pyrex or other microwave-safe bowl and microwave for 45 seconds, until the butter is completely melted. Pour the milk-butter mixture into the flour and lightly mix with a fork until it comes together into a dough. (NOTE: Don't overdo the mixing as that can make for a tough dumpling.) Use your hands to lightly knead the dough for 1 minute until it's smooth.

8 On a clean surface dusted lightly with flour, use a flour-coated rolling pin to roll the dough to ⅛ inch thick max. (NOTE: It's very important that it's no thicker than ⅛ inch to cook properly, as the dumplings will rise slightly.) Using a pizza cutter or knife, slice the dough vertically into strips about 1 inch wide and then horizontally about 2 inches apart to make little rectangular strips. Dust with additional flour so they don't stick to each other and gather on a plate.

CONTINUES

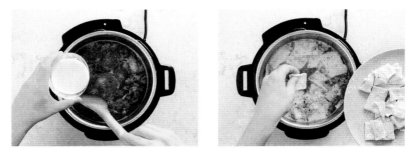

9 Make a cornstarch slurry by combining the cornstarch with 3 tablespoons cold water and set aside.

10 On the Instant Pot, hit Keep Warm/Cancel, then Sauté and Adjust so it's on the More or High setting. Once the broth mixture bubbles, immediately stir in the cornstarch slurry and add the dumpling strips one by one. Give them a good stir to be sure they aren't sticking together.

COMBINE THE CHICKEN & DUMPLINGS

11 Place the lid on the pot but do not seal it—just rest it off-kilter so steam is escaping from both sides. (Don't secure it as it may come to pressure even with the valve in the venting position.) Allow to simmer, covered, for 10 minutes.

12 Meanwhile, pick the chicken meat from the bones, discarding bones, skin, and cartilage. Rip the chicken into pieces by hand.

13 Once 10 minutes is up, hit Keep Warm/Cancel to turn off the heat. Add the chicken and heavy cream to the pot and stir until well combined. Allow to cool for 5 minutes and then ladle into bowls.

JEFF'S TIP **Want to leave out the dumplings completely to cut back on carbs? No problem. After adding the cornstarch slurry, just boil for a minute before killing the heat and adding the chicken and cream. You'll have the most amazing, creamy chicken soup instead!**

CHICKEN MARSALA

I can never pass up this classic Italian dish. Maybe it's the melty mushrooms. Maybe it's the dark, rich, wine-based sauce. Whatever the case, it's extra delicious when made in the Instant Pot.

Prep Time	Sauté Time	Pressure Building Time	Pressure Cook Time	Total Time	Serves
15 minutes	**20** minutes	**10–15** minutes	**8** minutes	**60** minutes	**4–6**

2   **pounds boneless, skinless chicken breasts, each breast sliced crosswise into fillets about ¼ inch thick**

½   **cup all-purpose flour (with a few pinches of garlic powder, black pepper, and kosher salt mixed in) for dredging**

¼   **cup extra-virgin olive oil**

4   **tablespoons (½ stick) salted butter, divided**

1   **shallot, minced**

3   **cloves garlic, minced or pressed**

1   **pound baby bella mushrooms, sliced**

¾   **cup Marsala wine (dry)**

½   **cup chicken broth**

1½ **tablespoons cornstarch**

1 Coat the chicken in the flour mixture and set aside.

2 Place the olive oil and 1 tablespoon of the butter in the Instant Pot. Hit Sauté and Adjust to the More or High setting and heat until the butter is melted.

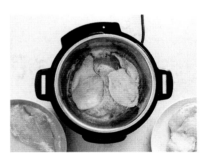

3 Working in batches, sear the chicken for 1 minute on each side until very lightly browned, remove the chicken with tongs, and set aside on a plate. Leave any excess oil in the pot for more flavor.

CONTINUES

4 Melt the remaining 3 tablespoons of butter in the pot—no need to wipe out any oil or flour left behind. Add the shallot and garlic and sauté, scraping up any browned bits from the bottom of the pot, for 2 minutes, then add the mushrooms and sauté for another 2 minutes.

5 Add the wine and give a final scrape to be sure the bottom of the pot is cleared. Add the chicken broth, then put the chicken back in the pot.

6 Secure the lid, move the valve to the sealing position, hit Keep Warm/Cancel, and then hit Manual or Pressure Cook on High Pressure for 8 minutes. Quick release when done.

7 Meanwhile, combine the cornstarch with 1½ tablespoons cold water to make a slurry. Set aside.

8 Remove the chicken to a serving platter and set aside, but leave the sauce in the pot. Hit Keep Warm/Cancel and then hit Sauté again and Adjust to More or High.

9 Once bubbling, immediately stir the cornstarch slurry into the sauce. Hit Keep Warm/Cancel to turn the pot off immediately.

10 Pour the sauce over the chicken and serve.

JEFF'S TIP Any leftover sauce goes great over rice or pasta and will keep in the fridge in an airtight container for up to 5 days.

MALL FOOD COURT
BOURBON
CHICKEN

OMG! Let's totally go to the mall food court and get free samples of bourbon chicken on a toothpick! On second thought, let's skip the crowds and just make it at home instead.

Prep Time	Sauté Time	Pressure Building Time	Pressure Cook Time	Total Time	Serves
5 minutes	**5** minutes	**10–15** minutes	**4** minutes	**30** minutes	**4–6**

2   tablespoons sesame oil
1   tablespoon salted butter
2   pounds boneless, skinless chicken thighs, cut into bite-size pieces
¼   cup bourbon

3   cloves garlic, minced or pressed
1   tablespoon minced ginger
⅓   cup chicken broth
¼   cup low-sodium soy sauce
¼   cup light-brown sugar

2   tablespoons rice vinegar or apple cider vinegar
2   tablespoons cornstarch
¼   cup ketchup
2   tablespoons hoisin sauce
2   tablespoons honey

1 Place the oil and butter in the Instant Pot, hit Sauté and Adjust so it's on the More or High setting, and allow it to heat up.

2 Once the butter's melted, add the chicken and sauté for 2 minutes until pinkish-white in color but not yet fully cooked.

3 Add the bourbon, garlic, and ginger and stir. Allow to simmer for another minute.

4 Add the broth, soy sauce, brown sugar, and vinegar. Stir well, secure the lid, move the valve to the sealing position, hit Keep Warm/Cancel, and then hit Pressure Cook or Manual on High Pressure for 4 minutes. Quick release when done.

5 Meanwhile, combine the cornstarch with 2 tablespoons cold water to form a slurry. Set aside.

6 When the lid comes off, stir in the ketchup, hoisin sauce, and honey.

7 Hit Keep Warm/Cancel and then hit Sauté and Adjust so it's on the More or High setting. Once it begins to bubble, immediately stir in the cornstarch slurry, allow to bubble, stirring occasionally, for 1 minute, then turn the pot off and let the sauce stand until thickened to your liking.

8 Serve over Hibachi Fried Rice (page 108) or White or Brown Rice (page 26).

 JEFF'S TIP If you want a thinner sauce, use only **1** tablespoon each of cornstarch and water.

CHICKEN & BROCCOLI

If you're craving this Chinese-American staple that combines chicken and broccoli coated in a savory, garlic-infused brown sauce, this recipe is going to satisfy you. Shaoxing rice wine can be found at most Asian markets, but you can also use cooking sherry.

Prep Time	Sauté Time	Pressure Building Time	Pressure Cook Time	Total Time	Serves
5 minutes	8 minutes	10–15 minutes	4 minutes	35 minutes	4–6

5 tablespoons sesame oil

1 tablespoon Shaoxing rice wine (or cooking sherry)

1 yellow onion, diced

1 bunch of scallions, thinly sliced

3 cloves garlic, minced or pressed

2 pounds boneless, skinless chicken breasts, cut into bite-size pieces

1 cup beef broth

¼ cup hoisin sauce

¼ cup low-sodium soy sauce

2 tablespoons oyster sauce

2 tablespoons dark-brown sugar

1–2 heads fresh broccoli, woody end of stalk trimmed and head cut into florets

2 tablespoons cornstarch

1 Place the oil and wine in the Instant Pot, hit Sauté and Adjust so it's on the More or High setting. Heat for 3 minutes.

2 Add the onion and scallions and cook for 2 minutes, until beginning to soften. Add the garlic and cook for 1 minute more.

3 Add the chicken and cook, stirring, until the edges are pinkish-white in color, but not yet fully cooked, about 1 minute. Add the beef broth, hoisin sauce, soy sauce, oyster sauce, and brown sugar and stir well to coat.

4 Secure the lid, move the valve to the sealing position, and hit Keep Warm/Cancel followed by Manual or Pressure Cook on High Pressure for 4 minutes. Quick release when done.

5 While the chicken is cooking, place the broccoli florets in a microwave-safe bowl and pour ¼ cup of water over them. Cover loosely with plastic wrap and microwave for 3–4 minutes, until slightly tender but still firm.

6 Mix the cornstarch with 2 tablespoons water to form a slurry. Set aside.

7 Once the pot has finished cooking, hit Keep Warm/Cancel and then hit Sauté again. When the sauce begins to bubble, immediately add in the cornstarch slurry and stir. Stir in the steamed broccoli and allow the liquid to simmer for 30 seconds, until thickened. Hit Keep Warm/Cancel to turn off the pot.

8 Serve with Hibachi Fried Rice (page 108) or White or Brown Rice (page 26).

 JEFF'S TIP Cooking the broccoli separately prevents it from becoming mushy or disintegrating under pressure in the Instant Pot.

CHICKEN SHAWARMA

When I was in the Middle East I had shawarma (a delicious pita sandwich made with roasted meats and various toppings) every day. When I got home, I created my own unconventional, yet authentic-tasting and addicting spin on this traditional recipe—and in the Instant Pot, it's so simple to make.

Prep Time	Sauté Time	Pressure Building Time	Pressure Cook Time	Total Time	Serves
5 minutes	**5** minutes	**10–15** minutes	**7** minutes	**30** minutes	**4–6**

½ cup extra-virgin olive oil

2 tablespoons (¼ stick) salted butter

1 yellow onion, sliced lengthwise into 1-inch wedges

3 cloves garlic, minced or pressed

4 pounds boneless, skinless chicken thighs, cut into ¼-inch strips

1 tablespoon paprika

1 tablespoon curry powder

1 tablespoon seasoned salt

2 teaspoons black pepper

1½ teaspoons ground cumin

1 teaspoon turmeric

1 teaspoon cinnamon

½–1 teaspoon cayenne pepper (optional)

½–1 teaspoon crushed red pepper flakes (optional)

½ cup garlic broth (e.g. Garlic Better Than Bouillon) or chicken broth

TO SERVE

Pita/flatbread, warmed or room temperature

Hummus (page 244)

Red onion, thinly sliced

Dill or sour pickles, diced

Tzatziki

1 Place the olive oil and butter in the Instant Pot, then hit Sauté and Adjust so it's on the More or High setting. Once the butter's melted, add the onion and garlic and sauté for about 3 minutes, until slightly softened.

2 Add the chicken thighs, paprika, curry powder, seasoned salt, black pepper, cumin, turmeric, cinnamon, cayenne pepper (if using), and crushed red pepper flakes (if using) and stir to coat everything in the spices.

3 Add the broth and stir well, scraping up any browned bits from the bottom of the pot.

4 Secure the lid, move the valve to the sealing position, hit Keep Warm/Cancel and then Manual or Pressure Cook on High Pressure for 7 minutes. Quick release when done.

5 Prepare your shawarma wrap and make it your own! I suggest you take some pita, spread on some hummus, and layer with chicken and onions from the pot as well as sliced red onion, pickles, and tzatziki. Finish by drizzling the incredible spice-infused oil from the pot over the top. Roll it up tightly (wrapping the sandwich in foil may help with any messy drippings) and enjoy!

JEFF'S TIP

The cooking liquid from the pot is also great for drizzling over rice and veggies!

CHICKEN ENCHILADA CASSEROLE

These dreamy chicken enchiladas are prepared casserole-style in a super cheesy sauce that will have you licking the plate. Feel free to top with some jalapeños for a fiesta of color.

Prep Time	Sauté Time	Pressure Building Time	Pressure Cook Time	Optional Oven Time	Total Time	Serves
5 minutes	**5** minutes	**10–15** minutes	**8** minutes	**20** minutes	**30–50** minutes	**4–6**

- **4 tablespoons (½ stick) salted butter**
- **¼ cup all-purpose flour**
- **2 cups chicken broth**
- **2 pounds boneless, skinless chicken thighs (or chicken breasts if you prefer)**

- **2 cups shredded Monterey Jack or Pepper Jack cheese**
- **10–12 small flour or corn tortillas (fajita size is the best for this)**
- **1 cup sour cream**
- **1 (7-ounce) can diced green chilies, with their juices (these aren't spicy)**

- **½ cup crumbled cotija cheese (use crumbled feta or grated Parmesan if you can't find cotija)**
- **1½ tablespoons cornstarch**
- **2 cups shredded Mexican cheese blend**

PREPARE THE CHICKEN

1 Place the butter in the Instant Pot and hit Sauté and Adjust so it's on the Less or Low setting.

2 Once the butter's melted, whisk in the flour and cook, whisking constantly, until just lightly browned, about 1 minute.

3 Add the chicken broth and stir and scrape up any browned bits from the bottom of the pot. Nestle the chicken thighs in the broth.

4 Secure the lid, move the valve to the sealing position, hit Keep Warm/Cancel and then Pressure Cook or Manual on High Pressure for 8 minutes. Quick release when done, remove the lid, hit Keep Warm/Cancel, and let the mixture stand to cool about 5 minutes.

5 Remove the chicken, place in a mixing bowl along with 2 tablespoons of the broth from the pot, and shred the meat using two forks (or a hand mixer). Let cool slightly, then add 2 cups of the Monterey Jack or Pepper Jack cheese. Mix together well.

ASSEMBLE THE ENCHILADAS

6 Using a ⅓-cup measuring cup, scoop the chicken-cheese mixture onto the tortillas and roll them up, leaving the ends open, and place in a 9 x 13-inch casserole dish, seam side down. (NOTE: If you plan on giving it a final bake in Step 11, prepare the dish with nonstick spray before adding the enchiladas.)

7 In the Instant Pot, whisk the sour cream into the broth until a smooth mixture forms. Once the sour cream and broth have come together, whisk in the green chilies and cotija cheese.

8 In a small bowl, mix the cornstarch with 1½ tablespoons cold water to form a slurry. Set aside.

9 On the Instant Pot, hit Sauté and Adjust so it's on the More or High setting. Once the broth mixture is bubbling, immediately stir in the cornstarch slurry and let cook for another minute until the sauce has thickened. Turn off the pot and let stand until thickened to your liking.

CONTINUES

10 Pour the sauce over the enchiladas and top with the 2 cups of shredded Mexican cheese before serving.

11 *Optional: For browner, meltier enchiladas,* bake in the oven at 350°F, uncovered, for 20 minutes, or until the cheese gets slightly browned.

 JEFF'S TIPS This dish goes great with my Refried Beans (page 242) or Tex-Mex Brown Rice and Beans (page 120).

Flour tortillas are a bit softer than corn tortillas. Choose your favorite—personally, I prefer flour.

While finishing the enchiladas in the oven is totally optional, I strongly recommend it for meltier, gooier cheese.

TURKEY BREAST & GRAVY

Who says it needs to be Thanksgiving to enjoy the tastiest, juiciest, tenderest turkey ever carved? Cooked in the Instant Pot, this turkey doesn't require constant basting or oven watching. You'll be able to gobble this one up any day of the week.

Prep Time	Sauté Time	Pressure Building Time	Pressure Cook Time	Natural Release Time	Optional Oven Time	Total Time	Serves
10 minutes	5 minutes	10–15 minutes	35 minutes	10 minutes	5–10 minutes	80 minutes	4–6

3   **tablespoons extra-virgin olive oil**

1   **tablespoon dried sage**

1   **teaspoon dried thyme**

1½ **teaspoons paprika**

1   **teaspoon dried tarragon**

1   **teaspoon seasoned salt**

2   **teaspoons pepper**

3   **cloves garlic, minced or pressed**

1   **(4–5 pound) turkey breast (bone-in or boneless), thawed, rinsed, and timer removed (if it came with one)**

2   **cups turkey or chicken broth**

1–2 **small yellow onions, quartered**

2   **large carrots, peeled and sliced into ½-inch disks**

3   **ribs celery, sliced**

2   **tablespoons cornstarch**

    A few drops Gravy Master or Kitchen Bouquet (optional)

2   **packets gravy mix (optional)**

1 In a bowl, mix together the olive oil, sage, thyme, paprika, tarragon, seasoned salt, pepper, and garlic. Set aside.

2 Place the turkey breast on the trivet, breast side up, and carefully lower into the pot using the handles. Use a silicone brush to apply the spice mixture all over the turkey.

3 Pour in the broth, then add the onions, carrots, and celery, arranging them around the side of the turkey breast (really stuff them in there as best you can).

CONTINUES

4 Secure the lid, move the valve to the sealing position, and hit Pressure Cook or Manual for 35 minutes on High Pressure. Allow a 10-minute natural release when done, followed by a quick release. Using the trivet's handles, transfer the turkey breast to a serving dish and leave everything else in the pot.

5 Meanwhile, mix the cornstarch with 2 tablespoons water to form a slurry. Set aside.

6 On the pot, hit Keep Warm/Cancel, then hit Sauté and Adjust to More or High, and stir in the Gravy Master (if using) and gravy packets (if using). Once the contents begin to bubble, immediately stir in the cornstarch slurry and simmer for 30 seconds. Turn the pot off by hitting Keep Warm/Cancel and let the gravy stand until thickened.

7 Carve the turkey into slices against the grain of the meat and serve, topped with the gravy.

JEFF'S TIPS

To really impress (which I strongly suggest), give this turkey breast some beautiful color and a slightly crisped skin. While the turkey's cooking in Step 4, preheat your oven to 400°F. When done pressure cooking, remove the turkey from the pot using the trivet's handles (leaving all the veggies in the pot) and transfer to a foil-lined baking sheet coated with nonstick spray. Dab the turkey with a little Gravy Master or Kitchen Bouquet (a little goes a long way so don't overdo it). Roast the turkey in the oven for 5–10 minutes, until golden. Keep an eye on it, as oven temperatures vary. Remove from the oven and allow to cool before carving.

IF USING THE INSTANT POT DUO CRISP, you can leave the turkey right in the pot while crisping! After Step 4, simply change the pressure cooking lid to the crisping lid, hit Air Fry at 400°F for 5–10 minutes, until golden, and then remove the turkey on the trivet and continue with Step 5.

CREAMY CURRY CHICKEN

Whenever I order Indian food, I can never decide on what to get because it's all so friggin' amazing. So I created a super-tender chicken dish with an irresistible rich and creamy tomato sauce peppered with glorious and easy-to-find spices. And it's so easy to make!

Prep Time	Sauté Time	Pressure Building Time	Pressure Cook Time	Total Time	Serves
5 minutes	10 minutes	10–15 minutes	8 minutes	40 minutes	4–6

8   tablespoons (1 stick) salted butter

1   large (or 2 medium) yellow onion, diced

6   cloves garlic, minced

½   tablespoon ginger, minced

3   pounds boneless, skinless chicken thighs, cut into bite-size pieces

1   tablespoon paprika

4   teaspoons garam masala, divided

1   teaspoon ground cumin

½   teaspoon turmeric

1½ teaspoons seasoned salt, divided

½   teaspoon cayenne pepper (optional)

1   (14.5-ounce) can diced tomatoes, with their juices

1   cup unsweetened coconut milk (it should be thin like water and not thick and lumpy)

½   cup Greek yogurt

2   tablespoons cornstarch

1   (6-ounce) can tomato paste

½   cup heavy cream
    Fresh cilantro, for serving
    Naan, for serving

1 Place the butter in the Instant Pot, then hit Sauté and Adjust so it's on the High or More setting.

2 Once the butter's melted, add the onion, garlic, and ginger and sauté for 5 minutes, until softened and beginning to brown slightly.

3 Add the chicken and sauté until the edges are pinkish-white in color, but not yet fully cooked, 2–3 minutes. Add the paprika, 3 teaspoons garam masala, cumin, turmeric, ½ teaspoon seasoned salt, and cayenne (if using) and sauté, stirring, for another minute.

4 Stir in the diced tomatoes and coconut milk and top off with the Greek yogurt, but *do not stir in the yogurt!* Simply let it rest on top of everything else in the pot.

5 Secure the lid, move the valve to the sealing position, and hit Keep Warm/Cancel followed by Manual or Pressure Cook on High Pressure for 8 minutes. Quick release when done. Meanwhile, mix the cornstarch with 2 tablespoons water to form a slurry. Set aside.

6 Stir in the tomato paste, cream, the remaining teaspoon of garam masala, and the remaining teaspoon of seasoned salt. Hit Keep Warm/Cancel followed by Sauté and Adjust so it's on More or High. Once bubbling, immediately stir in the cornstarch slurry and simmer for 30 seconds before hitting Keep Warm/Cancel to turn the pot off. Allow to sit for 5 minutes to thicken.

7 Serve with cilantro and naan, if desired.

 JEFF'S TIP In Step 6, add half a package (3 ounces) of Boursin spread, any flavor, for an extra-creamy consistency.

CHICKEN SCARPARIELLO

"Chicken Scarpariello" sounds like a famous Italian chicken opera singer. And that's fitting since your mouth will be hitting high notes once you try it. Chicken paired with Italian sausage in a sweet onion and red pepper Marsala sauce is what sets the stage for this fabulous night at home.

Prep Time	Sauté Time	Pressure Building Time	Pressure Cook Time	Total Time	Serves
5 minutes	15 minutes	10–15 minutes	6 minutes	45 minutes	4–6

¼ cup extra-virgin olive oil

3 pounds boneless or bone-in, skinless chicken thighs

4 tablespoons (½ stick) salted butter

1 large Vidalia (sweet) onion, diced

1 pound baby bella mushrooms, sliced

6 cloves garlic, minced

1 pound sweet or hot Italian sausage, with casings, sliced into ½-inch-thick pieces

¾ cup Marsala wine (dry)

¼ cup chicken broth

1 teaspoon dried rosemary

1 teaspoon dried thyme

1 teaspoon Italian seasoning

1 teaspoon seasoned salt

2½ tablespoons cornstarch

¼ cup heavy cream or half-and-half

1 (12-ounce) jar roasted red peppers, drained and sliced into ¼-inch strips

½ cup grated Parmesan cheese

1 On the Instant Pot, hit Sauté and Adjust so it's on the High or More setting. Pour in the olive oil and heat about 3 minutes. In batches, add the chicken and sauté for 30 seconds on each side until lightly seared but not cooked, constantly moving the thighs around so they don't stick to the pot too much (it's fine if some do). When done, transfer the chicken to a plate to rest.

2 Add the butter and onion, and as the butter melts, scrape the bottom of the pot of most chicken bits. Add the mushrooms and garlic and sauté for 3 minutes, until just softened.

3 Add the sausage and sauté for 2 minutes.

JEFF'S TIP I prefer a sear of the chicken directly in the olive oil in Step 1 as written. However, if you don't want to deal with the chicken sticking to the pot and having to move it around constantly as you flash-sear, add in 2 additional tablespoons of butter with the oil.

4 Pour in the Marsala wine and bring to a simmer, once more scraping the bottom of the pot to free it of most browned bits. Stir in the broth, rosemary, thyme, Italian seasoning, and seasoned salt. Place the chicken back in the pot, resting on top of everything.

5 Secure the lid, move the valve to the sealing position, and hit Keep Warm/Cancel followed by Manual or Pressure Cook on High Pressure for 6 minutes. Quick release when done. Use tongs to remove the chicken to a serving dish to rest.

6 Make a cornstarch slurry by mixing the cornstarch with 2½ tablespoons cold water. Set aside.

7 Stir in the cream and roasted red peppers. Hit Keep Warm/Cancel and then Sauté and Adjust so it's on the High or More setting. Once it begins to bubble, immediately stir in the cornstarch slurry and Parmesan. Let simmer for 30 seconds, turn off the pot, and let stand for 5 minutes to let the sauce thicken before draping over the chicken.

JEFF'S TIPS

This goes wonderfully over long noodles, such as linguine, fettuccine, or capellini/angel hair.

A great way to slice raw sausage links easily is to pop them in the freezer for 5 minutes before slicing. They hold their form much better this way!

TANGY CHICKEN WINGS

This recipe is as if Baby Back Ribs took the day off, letting their friend Chicken shine in an incredible homemade barbecue sauce. These wings ain't only juicy, they're bursting with tangy flavor.

Prep Time	Sauté Time	Pressure Building Time	Pressure Cook Time	Optional Oven Time	Total Time	Serves
5 minutes	3 minutes	10–15 minutes	8 minutes	5–10 minutes	35 minutes	4–6

1 cup ketchup

1 cup apple cider vinegar

1 cup packed light-brown sugar

⅓ cup yellow mustard

1 tablespoon onion powder

1 teaspoon garlic powder

½ teaspoon chili powder

¼ teaspoon salt

1 tablespoon honey

3 pounds chicken wings/wingettes/drumettes

2 tablespoons cornstarch

 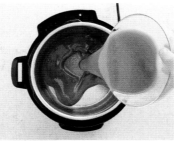 

1 In a mixing bowl, whisk together the ketchup, vinegar, brown sugar, mustard, onion powder, garlic powder, chili powder, salt, and honey and pour into the Instant Pot.

2 Turn the Instant Pot on Sauté and Adjust so it's on the More or High setting. Bring the mixture just to a simmer and hit Keep Warm/Cancel. Add the trivet to the pot and rest the wings on it (they can rest on top of each other).

JEFF'S TIPS

These go amazingly with my Premium Potato Salad (page 236).

Don't feel like broiling the wings for a crisped touch? Serve as is after basting the wings with the sauce.

3 Secure the lid, move the valve to the sealing position, and hit Manual or Pressure Cook on High Pressure for 8 minutes. Quick release when done.

4 Mix the cornstarch with 2 tablespoons water to form a slurry. Set aside.

5 Using tongs, transfer the wings to a foil-lined baking sheet, remove the trivet, and then hit Keep Warm/Cancel and then Sauté again and bring that amazing tangy BBQ sauce to a bubble. Once it does, immediately stir in the cornstarch slurry, mix well, and let bubble for 30 seconds.

6 Hit Keep Warm/Cancel to turn the heat off and let the sauce cool for 5 minutes until it stops bubbling and thickens nicely.

7 Brush the sauce on the wings and, for optimal results, I recommend you broil in the oven for 5–10 minutes until slightly crisped and caramelized. If using an Instant Pot Duo Crisp, you can do this directly in the pot by adding the crisping lid and hitting Broil at 400°F for 5–10 minutes, flipping midway through until the desired crispiness is achieved.

CHICKEN À LA QUEENS

This dish is comfort food at its finest. It's almost like a chicken pot pie without the crust. A traditional chicken à la king calls for a sauce thickened with a roux (a fancy word for flour and fat), but being a fella with no limits (who lives in Queens), I decided to give this sauce its creamy texture with herb cream cheese, and I swapped out the pimentos for roasted red peppers. And thus chicken à la king becomes Chicken à la Queens.

Prep Time	Sauté Time	Pressure Building Time	Pressure Cook Time	Total Time	Serves
5 minutes	**8** minutes	**10–15** minutes	**4** minutes	**30** minutes	**4–6**

4 tablespoons (½ stick) salted butter

1 pound baby bella mushrooms, sliced

1 large shallot, diced

1 yellow bell pepper, diced

3 pounds boneless, skinless chicken breasts, cut into bite-size pieces

1 cup chicken broth

1 teaspoon garlic powder

1 teaspoon seasoned salt

1 teaspoon black pepper

½ cup heavy cream or half-and-half

1 (5.2-ounce) package Boursin spread (any flavor) or 4 ounces cream cheese, cut into chunky cubes

1 cup frozen peas

1 (12-ounce) jar roasted red peppers, drained and sliced into ¼-inch strips

2 tablespoons cornstarch

1 cup grated Parmesan cheese

Canned biscuits of your choice, cooked according to package instructions, for serving

1 Place the butter in the Instant Pot and hit Sauté and Adjust so it's on High or More setting. Once the butter's melted, add the mushrooms, shallot, and bell pepper and sauté for 3 minutes until slightly softened.

2 Add the chicken and sauté for 2–3 minutes, until the chicken is lightly seared and the edges are pinkish-white in color, but not yet fully cooked. Stir in the chicken broth, garlic powder, seasoned salt, and pepper.

3 Secure the lid, move the valve to the sealing position, and hit Keep Warm/Cancel followed by Manual or Pressure Cook on High Pressure for 4 minutes. Quick release when done.

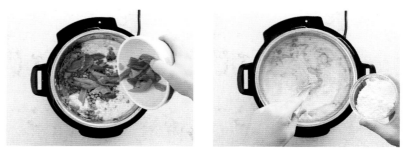

4 Mix the cornstarch with 2 tablespoons water to form a slurry. Set aside.

5 Stir in the cream, Boursin (or cream cheese), frozen peas, and roasted red peppers and let sit for a minute, stirring occasionally (the residual heat will thaw the peas). Hit Keep Warm/Cancel and then Sauté and Adjust to More or High. Once the sauce is bubbling, immediately stir in the cornstarch slurry and Parmesan and let bubble for 30 seconds before turning the pot off by hitting Keep Warm/Cancel again.

6 Serve over biscuits.

JEFF'S TIP

Don't care for peas? Okay! Use 1 cup of any frozen veggie mix to take their place.

CHICKEN OREGANATA

This chicken adorned with a lemony, buttery, garlicky sauce and topped with breadcrumbs is so delectable, you'll get verklempt.

Prep Time	Sauté Time	Pressure Building Time	Pressure Cook Time	Oven Time	Total Time	Serves
5 minutes	20 minutes	5–10 minutes	5 minutes	2–3 minutes	45 minutes	4–6

2 pounds boneless, skinless chicken breasts, each breast sliced crosswise into fillets about ¼ inch thick

½ cup all-purpose flour (seasoned with a pinch each of garlic powder, salt, and pepper)

¼ cup extra-virgin olive oil

4 tablespoons (½ stick) salted butter, divided

2 large shallots, diced

3 cloves garlic, minced or pressed

½ cup dry white wine (like a chardonnay)

Juice of 1 lemon

¾ cup garlic broth (e.g. Garlic Better Than Bouillon) or chicken broth

2 teaspoons dried oregano, plus more for topping

½ teaspoon kosher salt

½ teaspoon black pepper

1 tablespoon cornstarch

1 (14-ounce) can artichoke hearts, drained and quartered

¼ cup Italian or garlic-and-herb breadcrumbs

¼ cup grated Parmesan cheese

1 Dredge the chicken on both sides in the flour mixture and set aside.

2 Pour the olive oil and 2 tablespoons of the butter in the Instant Pot and hit Sauté and Adjust so it's on the More or High setting, and heat about 3 minutes, until the butter's melted.

3 Working in batches, sear the chicken for 1 minute on each side until very lightly browned, remove the chicken with tongs, and set aside on a plate. Leave any excess oil in the pot for more flavor.

CONTINUES

4 Add the remaining 2 tablespoons of butter and scrape up any browned bits from the bottom of the pot. Add the shallots and sauté for about 2 minutes, until beginning to brown, then add the garlic and sauté for 1 more minute. Add the wine and lemon juice and bring to a simmer.

5 Add the broth, oregano, kosher salt, and pepper and stir well, giving the bottom of the pot one last scrape for good measure. Return the chicken to the pot.

6 Secure the lid, move the valve to the sealing position, and hit Keep Warm/Cancel and then Manual or Pressure Cook on High Pressure for 5 minutes. Quick release when done and preheat the oven to broil.

7 Mix the cornstarch with 1 tablespoon water to form a slurry. Set aside.

JEFF'S TIP

There will be some excess sauce. Good! It's amazing over pasta, rice, on bread—you name it!

8 When the pot is done cooking, remove the lid and transfer the chicken to a casserole dish. Hit Keep Warm/Cancel and then hit Sauté and Adjust so it's on the More or High setting. Once the sauce bubbles, immediately add the cornstarch slurry and stir for 30 seconds, as the sauce thickens. Then hit Keep Warm/Cancel, and once the bubbles die down, the sauce will have thickened beautifully. Stir in the artichokes and then pour the sauce over the chicken in the casserole dish.

9 Once the broiler is heated, mix the breadcrumbs and Parmesan, sprinkle evenly over the chicken and top with a few more shakes of oregano. Place the casserole dish on the top rack of the oven and broil for 2–3 minutes (keep an eye on it, as oven temperatures vary and we don't want the breadcrumbs to burn). Remove and serve immediately over rice or angel-hair pasta (cooked separately), if you wish. And of course, get some Italian or French bread to dip in that remarkable sauce.

MÉNAGE À
THAI
CHICKEN CURRY

(CURRY THREE WAYS)

I could eat Thai food every day. When it comes to Thai curry, I can never choose between green, red, or massaman. It's like choosing your favorite child. This simple base recipe lets you make any of the three with just a few simple modifications. After giving this a whirl, you just may never order takeout again!

Prep Time	Sauté Time	Pressure Building Time	Pressure Cook Time	Total Time	Serves
5 minutes	**15** minutes	**5–10** minutes	**6** minutes	**40** minutes	**4–6**

2   tablespoons vegetable oil

1   large yellow onion, sliced lengthwise into ¼-inch pieces

1   large green bell pepper, cut in half lengthwise and then into ½-inch-thick slices

8   ounces green beans, ends trimmed

3   cloves garlic, minced or pressed

1   tablespoon ginger, minced or crushed

2   pounds boneless, skinless chicken breasts, sliced crosswise into ¼-inch thick fillets then cut into bite-size pieces

¼   cup Thai basil or tarragon, plus more for serving

1   (14-ounce) can unsweetened coconut milk (it should be thin like water and not thick and lumpy)

4   ounces red, green, or massaman curry paste, divided (see Jeff's Tip)

1   tablespoon light-brown sugar

1   teaspoon cumin

1   teaspoon coriander

Juice of 1 lime

3   tablespoons fish sauce

1   (8-ounce) can bamboo shoots, drained

2   tablespoons cornstarch (optional, for a thicker curry)

JEFF'S TIP

Curry paste can be found in the Asian section of most markets or online. Depending on which curry paste you use, you'll do the following. Cook time will remain the same for all:

• **GREEN CURRY** (medium spice)—Follow recipe exactly as is.

• **RED CURRY** (very spicy)—You can keep the green bell pepper or substitute a red bell pepper and add ¼ teaspoon cayenne pepper when adding the spices in Step 3.

• **MASSAMAN CURRY** (mild, peanut flavored)—Omit the green bell pepper and add 1 diced and peeled potato and 1 diced carrot in Step 3, and add ⅓ cup chunky or smooth peanut butter and stir until blended in Step 5. Serve topped with peanuts, if desired.

CONTINUES

1 Pour the vegetable oil into the Instant Pot, hit Sauté and Adjust so it's on More or High, and heat about 3 minutes. Add the onion, bell pepper, and green beans and sauté for 5 minutes, until slightly softened. Add the garlic and ginger and cook for 1 minute longer.

2 Add the chicken and Thai basil and sauté until pinkish-white in color but not fully cooked, about 3 minutes.

3 Add the coconut milk and stir, scraping up any bits from the bottom of the pot. Add 3 tablespoons of the curry paste, then the brown sugar, cumin, coriander, lime juice, fish sauce, and bamboo shoots and stir well.

4 Secure the lid, move the valve to the sealing position, and hit Keep Warm/Cancel and then Manual or Pressure Cook on High Pressure for 6 minutes. Quick release when done.

5 Stir in the remaining curry paste and let stand for 5 minutes.

6 *For an optional, thicker curry, before serving:* Mix the cornstarch with 2 tablespoons water to form a slurry. Hit Keep Warm/Cancel and then hit Sauté and Adjust to More or High. Once bubbling, add the slurry and immediately stir for 30 seconds before hitting Keep Warm/Cancel to turn the pot off.

7 Serve over jasmine or brown rice, topped with additional Thai basil or tarragon.

FIESTA
CHICKEN
TACOS

Even when the maracas start shaking and the margaritas flow, it's not a fiesta until you've had tacos! This ridiculously easy Mexican-inspired dish features a wonderful salsa base dressed up for that perfect south-of-the-border flavor.

Prep Time	Pressure Building Time	Pressure Cook Time	Total Time	Serves
3	**5–10**	**12**	**25**	**4–6**
minutes	minutes	minutes	minutes	

THE FIESTA CHICKEN

1   (16-ounce) jar red salsa (use your favorite)

1   cup chicken broth

¼   cup taco sauce (such as Old El Paso)

1   (1-ounce) packet taco seasoning

1   teaspoon garlic powder

1   teaspoon Goya sazón seasoning (optional)

2   pounds boneless, skinless chicken breasts

10–12 tortillas or taco shells

THE TACO FIXIN'S

Sour cream

Guacamole

Shredded cheese

Diced tomatoes

1 Stir together the salsa, chicken broth, taco sauce, taco seasoning, garlic powder, and sazón seasoning (if using) in the Instant Pot. Add the chicken breasts.

2 Secure the lid, move the valve to the sealing position, and hit Manual or Pressure Cook on High Pressure for 12 minutes. Quick release when done.

3 Place the chicken in a bowl and shred it using two forks (or a hand mixer to really make it easy).

4 After the chicken is shredded, mix in as much of the sauce as you'd like to keep the chicken moist and juicy. Serve with tortillas or taco shells and your favorite taco fixings—like sour cream, shredded cheese, guacamole, tomatoes, and more of the fiesta sauce the chicken cooked in.

JEFF'S TIPS

Got extra sauce? Let it flow over my **Tex-Mex Rice and Beans (page 120)!**

If using very thick breasts, slice them in half before pressure cooking. If you decide not to, pressure cook for 17 minutes to ensure they're cooked through.

CHICKEN FETA FLORENTINE

After a recent trip to Italy and Greece, I was inspired to create this dish, which combines the flavors of each! This creamy garlic sauce filled with spinach and feta cheese may just transport you to Tuscany, the Acropolis, or both!

Prep Time	Sauté Time	Pressure Building Time	Pressure Cook Time	Total Time	Serves
5 minutes	20 minutes	5–10 minutes	5 minutes	40 minutes	4–6

2   pounds boneless, skinless chicken breasts, sliced crosswise into fillets about ¼ inch thick

½   cup all-purpose flour (with some garlic powder, salt, and pepper sprinkled in)

¼   cup extra-virgin olive oil

4   tablespoons (½ stick) salted butter, divided

1   large shallot, diced

3   cloves garlic, minced or pressed

½   cup dry white wine (like a sauvignon blanc)

Juice of 1 lemon

½   cup garlic broth (e.g. Garlic Better Than Bouillon) or chicken broth

2   teaspoons dried parsley

1   teaspoon kosher salt

1   teaspoon black pepper

8–12 ounces baby spinach

½   cup heavy cream

1   (5.2-ounce) package Boursin spread (any flavor) or 4 ounces cream cheese, cut into chunky cubes

1   cup crumbled feta cheese, plus extra for serving

1 Dredge the chicken on both sides in the flour mixture and set aside.

2 Pour the olive oil and 2 tablespoons of the butter into the Instant Pot, hit Sauté and Adjust so it's on the More or High setting, and heat about 3 minutes. Working in batches so as not to crowd the pot, sear the chicken for 1 minute on each side until very lightly browned. Remove from the pot and set aside.

3 Add the remaining 2 tablespoons of butter to the pot, and once it melts, scrape up any browned bits or flour from the bottom of the pot. Add the shallot and sauté for about 2 minutes, until lightly brown, then add the garlic and sauté for another minute. Pour in the white wine and lemon juice and simmer for 1 minute longer.

4 Add the broth, parsley, kosher salt, and pepper. Stir well, scraping the bottom of the pot again, then add the chicken back to the pot and top it off with the spinach, but *do not stir*. Just lay the spinach on top and push it down gently with your hand. It's going to come to the brim, but don't worry—it will cook down significantly.

5 Secure the lid, move the valve to the sealing position, hit Keep Warm/Cancel and then hit Manual or Pressure Cook on High Pressure for 5 minutes. Quick release when done.

6 Move the spinach aside and transfer the chicken pieces to a serving dish. Stir the cream, Boursin or cream cheese, and feta into the sauce. To serve, pour the sauce over the chicken and top with extra feta.

JEFF'S TIP **This pairs perfectly with my Avgolemono Soup (page 60) or Sausage & Spinach Soup (page 52).**

BUFFALO CHICKEN WRAPS

I'm absolutely addicted to Buffalo chicken. I'd drink the sauce from the bottle (no judging, okay?). Here, we glorify basic shredded chicken by adding some magical Buffalo sauce to it. This dish is so crazy delicious, it's a good thing it's so easy!

Prep Time	Pressure Building Time	Pressure Cook Time	Total Time	Serves
2 minutes	**5–10** minutes	**12** minutes	**25** minutes	**4–6**

1 cup chicken broth

2 pounds boneless, skinless chicken breasts

1 cup Buffalo sauce of your choice

TO SERVE

6–8 tortillas, butter lettuce, or your favorite wraps

Buttermilk Ranch Dressing (recipe follows) or bottled blue cheese dressing

Blue cheese crumbles for topping (optional)

1 Place the broth and chicken in the Instant Pot.

2 Secure the lid, move the valve to the sealing position, and hit Manual or Pressure Cook on High Pressure for 12 minutes. Quick release when done.

3 Transfer the chicken to a bowl, add ¼ cup of the cooking liquid from the pot, and shred the chicken using two forks (or a hand mixer to really make it easy).

4 Mix in the Buffalo sauce and serve with your favorite wrap or sandwich fixings. For added zing, top with my Buttermilk Ranch dressing or bottled blue cheese dressing, and sprinkle with blue cheese crumbles.

 JEFF'S TIP If using very thick breasts, slice them in half before pressure cooking. If you don't, pressure cook for 17 minutes to ensure they're cooked through.

BUTTERMILK RANCH DRESSING

½ cup mayonnaise

½ cup sour cream

½ cup buttermilk

2 teaspoons white vinegar

1½ teaspoons dried dill

½ teaspoon dried parsley

½ teaspoon dried cilantro

½ teaspoon garlic powder

¼ teaspoon onion powder

¼ teaspoon seasoned salt

¼ teaspoon black pepper

½ cup crumbled blue cheese
(if you want to make it blue
cheese–style)

Whisk together all the ingredients in a bowl and chill for 1 hour before serving. Dressing will keep in an airtight container in the fridge for up to 2 weeks.

MEAT

Typically, a centerpiece roast or special-occasion meat dish can take hours when braised, slow-cooked, or roasted in the oven. That's all history now, because the Instant Pot gives you tender, flavorful, and melt-in-your-mouth-like-butta roasts and braises that come together in moments.

Best-Ever Pot
Roast
172

Barbecue Ribs
175

Jewish Brisket
178

Beef Stroganoff
181

Meatloaf &
Mashed Potatoes
184

Corned Beef &
Cabbage
187

Orange Sesame
Beef
190

Pulled Pork
192

Swedish
Meatballs
194

Spiced Short
Ribs
196

Sausage
& Peppers
Parmesan
198

Dijon Dill Pork
Tenderloin
200

Hungarian
Goulash
202

Shepherd's Pie
204

BEST-EVER POT ROAST

Behold. This is my very most popular recipe, and you're about to find out why. This fork-tender roast also makes a gravy so delicious, you'll want to lap it up with some rice and crusty bread (or just a spoon).

Prep Time	Sauté Time	Pressure Building Time	Pressure Cook Time	Natural Release Time	Total Time	Serves
15 minutes	15 minutes	10–20 minutes	60 minutes	15 minutes	2 hours	4–6

2 teaspoons black pepper

1½ teaspoons kosher salt

1½ teaspoons seasoned salt

1½ teaspoons dried parsley

1 teaspoon dried thyme

1 teaspoon dried rosemary

1 teaspoon onion powder

1 teaspoon garlic powder

1 (3-pound) chuck roast

3 tablespoons extra-virgin olive oil

1 tablespoon salted butter

2 medium yellow onions, sliced into thick wedges

3 cloves garlic, sliced

2 tablespoons Worcestershire sauce

1 cup dry red wine (like a cabernet)

6–8 ounces portobello mushrooms, sliced

2 cups beef broth

8 ounces fresh baby carrots

1 pound baby white potatoes

3 tablespoons cornstarch

1 packet beef gravy mix

1 Mix together the pepper, kosher salt, seasoned salt, parsley, thyme, rosemary, onion powder, and garlic powder and rub the mix into the roast on all sides.

2 On the Instant Pot, hit Sauté and Adjust to the More or High setting. Pour in the oil and heat for 3 minutes, then sear the seasoned roast in the pan without moving it for about 1–2 minutes on each side. Remove the roast from the pot and set aside.

3 Without wiping out the liner pot, put the butter in the Instant Pot, and as it melts use a wooden spoon to scrape up any spices stuck to the bottom. Add the onions and cook for 2 minutes, continuing to stir and scrape up any browned bits. Add the garlic and Worcestershire sauce and continue to stir and scrape for another minute until the bottom of the pot is smooth.

CONTINUES

JEFF'S TIP While most recipes keep the cooking time the same if doubling recipes, roasts are an exception. Since roasts are thick, adjust the cooking time per pound of meat. For this pot roast, cook at 60 minutes for 3 pounds, 70 minutes for 4 pounds, and 80 minutes for 5 pounds. Allow a 15-minute natural release regardless of the roast's size. But always use fresh (not frozen) meat for this recipe.

4 Place the trivet over the onions with the handles facing upward, then add the wine and place the roast on top of the trivet, fat side up (so the juices will run through the meat as it cooks), and fill in the mushrooms around the sides. Pour the beef broth on top.

5 Wrap the potatoes and carrots each in their own foil pouches and place in the pot on top of the roast. It's okay if you have to move things around to make room.

6 Secure the lid, move the valve to the sealing position, hit Keep Warm/Cancel and then hit Pressure Cook or Manual on High Pressure for 60 minutes (see Jeff's Tip for cook times for larger roasts). When done, use a natural release for 15 minutes, and then a quick release.

7 Meanwhile, make a cornstarch slurry by mixing the cornstarch with 3 tablespoons of cold water and set aside.

8 Once the pot has finished cooking, remove the foil-wrapped veggies and set aside. Carefully remove the roast and the trivet and let the meat rest on a cutting board.

9 Press Keep Warm/Cancel and then Sauté and Adjust so it's on the More or High setting and bring the sauce to a simmer. Unwrap the veggies and stir them into the sauce along with the cornstarch slurry and gravy packet. Let simmer for 30 seconds and then turn the pot to the Keep Warm setting.

10 Using a sharp knife, slice the pot roast against the grain in strips about ¼ inch thick (or make thicker or bite-size cuts if you wish). Then, add them into the sauce (still on the Keep Warm setting). Make sure you toss in any remaining little strands of meat from your cutting board and give everything a final stir, then serve.

BARBECUE RIBS

Prepare yourselves for ribs so stupendous and succulent, they'll strip right off the bone into your mouth. Whether baby back or St. Louis–style, ribs have never been so perfect or easy to make.

Prep Time	Pressure Building Time	Pressure Cook Time	Natural Release Time	Optional Oven Time	Total Time varies, but typically	Serves
5 minutes	**20–30** minutes	**18–30** minutes	**5** minutes	**10** minutes	**80** minutes	**4–6**

2–6 pounds (up to 3 full racks) of St. Louis or baby back ribs (pork loin back ribs), unseasoned

1 (64-ounce) bottle of apple juice (NOTE: You can halve this or even reduce to only 2 cups. I just like to use the full bottle so all the meat gets infused.)

1 cup apple cider vinegar

¼ cup liquid smoke (either hickory or mesquite is fine)

Barbecue sauce (a few cups' worth)

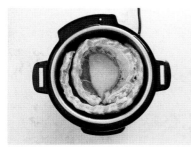

1 Take the ribs and coil them so they fit in the Instant Pot lined against the perimeter of the pot. A 6-quart should be able to handle up to 2 racks of ribs, while the 8-quart can handle 3 full racks. If you wish to cut each rack in half before inserting for easier removal once cooked, feel free to do so.

2 Add the apple juice, vinegar, and liquid smoke.

3 Secure the lid, move the valve to the sealing position, and hit Manual or Pressure Cook on High Pressure for 30 minutes for 5–6 pounds/1.5–2 racks of ribs (25 minutes for 2–4 pounds/1 rack). If you want the ribs slightly firmer, go for only 23 minutes for 5–6 pounds/1.5–2 racks of ribs (18 minutes for 2–4 pounds/1 rack). *However,* I do recommend you go for the longer cooking time in order to achieve that super-tender, fall-off-the-bone bite. (NOTE: The pot may take about 20 minutes to come to pressure due to the amount of liquid inside. You aren't doing anything wrong!)

CONTINUES

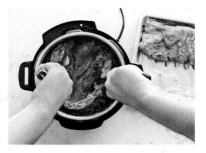

4 When done, allow a 5-minute natural release followed by a quick release. (NOTE: If it splatters while releasing, you can throw a dish towel on top of the nozzle to absorb any splatter or allow a full natural release, meaning you never turn the release nozzle and let it release on its own until the pin drops.)

5 Since the ribs are going to be super tender, *carefully* remove them from the pot to a baking sheet lined with nonstick foil (bone side down). I use two sets of tongs to make this happen, but it's okay if the rack splits in half when being moved—just try to be delicate. Discard the juices from the pot after the ribs are removed (or use it again if you immediately want to make more ribs!).

6 Using a basting brush, generously coat the tops of the ribs with the barbecue sauce. Slather it on real good so they're pretty and saucy!

7 *For optimal results*, pop the sauced ribs on the foil-lined baking sheet in a preheated oven at 400°F, and cook for 10 minutes. The sauce will caramelize onto the ribs.

8 Remove the ribs from the oven, slice them up, grab lots of napkins, and enjoy!

JEFF'S TIPS

If you have a grill, feel free to throw the sauced ribs on it to make them extra crispy instead of finishing in the oven. But be careful: these ribs are *super* tender and can easily come apart if handled roughly!

If you wish to make barbecue sauce, try the one I use in my Tangy Chicken Wings recipe (page 154).

This goes great with my Mac & Cheese (page 32) or Premium Potato Salad (page 236)!

JEWISH BRISKET

I take such pride in this dish. To me, being Jewish is all about traditions, and in Jewish families, brisket is a tradition in and of itself. We're talking tender, fall-apart brisket in an incredibly simple sweet and savory sauce (trust me on the ketchup). But food knows no religion. In fact, a few of my goyim friends now include this Jewish Brisket on their Christmas and Easter tables!

Prep Time	Sauté Time	Pressure Building Time	Pressure Cook Time	Natural Release Time	Total Time	Serves
5 minutes	5 minutes	10–15 minutes	65–75 minutes	20 minutes	2 hours	4–6

1 (4- or 5-pound) beef brisket (don't trim the fat prior to cooking)
   Kosher salt

1½ cups water
1½ cups ketchup
¾ cup dark-brown sugar
¾ cup white vinegar

1 clove garlic, minced or pressed
4 yellow onions, coarsely chopped
3 tablespoons cornstarch

1 Take the brisket and cut it in half against the grain so it fits into your Instant Pot. Rub the brisket all over with kosher salt.

2 On the Instant Pot, hit Sauté and Adjust so it's on the More or High setting. Once it says Hot, working with one piece at a time, sear the brisket for 2 minutes on each side, or until browned. When done, hit Keep Warm/Cancel, move the brisket to a plate, and clean and dry the liner pot.

3 Make the sauce by whisking together the water, ketchup, brown sugar, vinegar, and garlic in a mixing bowl.

CONTINUES

JEFF'S TIPS

If using a 2–3-pound brisket, reduce the pressure cooking time to 55–60 minutes.

Brisket tastes even better the next day. The day or night before you wish to serve it, make the recipe and then, once sliced, transfer the brisket and the sauce to an aluminum pan and refrigerate, covered with aluminum foil, overnight. When you're ready to serve, reheat the whole pan with the foil on top in the oven for about 30 minutes at 350°F.

4 With the liner pot and the trivet in the Instant Pot, place one half of the brisket on top of the trivet, fat-side up, and cover with about half of the onions and sauce. Then, in crisscross fashion, layer the other half of the brisket (also fat-side up) on top of the onions. Cover the brisket with the remaining onions and sauce.

5 Secure the lid, move the valve to the sealing position, and hit Manual or Pressure Cook on High Pressure for 75 minutes if you want it super tender (shredding apart) or 65 minutes if you want it a little firmer. When done, allow a 20-minute natural release followed by a quick release.

6 Very carefully transfer the brisket halves to a carving board (placing them fat side up) and let cool for 15 minutes. If you decide to carve it up into strips right away before it's done cooling, it will shred apart. While you wait, you may carefully shave off any undesired fat and discard (or keep it on if you wish).

7 Meanwhile, as the brisket's cooling, mix the cornstarch with 3 tablespoons cold water to form a slurry and set aside.

8 Hit Keep Warm/Cancel and then Sauté and Adjust to the High or More setting to bring the sauce to a simmer. Add the slurry, stir immediately, and allow it to simmer for 30 seconds before turning the pot to the Keep Warm setting. The sauce will thicken as the brisket cools.

9 Once the brisket has cooled, use a carving knife to cut it into strips or chunks, slicing against the grain (meaning the opposite direction that the strings of meat are going in).

10 Carefully return the slices of meat to the Instant Pot and allow to marinate in the sauce (on the Keep Warm setting) for 5–10 minutes, so it stays tender until ready to serve.

BEEF STROGANOFF

One of my most popular and lauded recipes, this Beef Stroganoff is going to ruin all others for you. Find out why.

Prep Time	Sauté Time	Pressure Building Time	Pressure Cook Time	Natural Release Time	Total Time	Serves
5 minutes	**10** minutes	**10–15** minutes	**20** minutes	**10** minutes	**60** minutes	**4–6**

3 **pounds beef stew meat or chuck cubes**

Kosher salt and black pepper, to season beef (1–2 teaspoons of each)

3 **tablespoons extra-virgin olive oil**

5 **tablespoons salted butter, divided**

1 **large yellow onion, diced**

1 **pound baby bella mushrooms, sliced**

3 **cloves garlic, minced or pressed**

¼ **cup dry white wine (like a sauvignon blanc)**

1 **tablespoon Dijon mustard**

1 **teaspoon seasoned salt**

1½ **cups beef broth**

1 **teaspoon dried thyme**

4 **tablespoons cornstarch**

1 **packet dry onion soup/dip mix**

1 **cup sour cream**

1 **(5.2-ounce) package Boursin spread (any flavor) or 4 ounces cream cheese, cut into chunky cubes**

1 **(12-ounce) package wide egg noodles, prepared separately according to package directions**

1 Season the meat all over with kosher salt and black pepper and rub it in well.

2 Place the olive oil and 2 tablespoons of the butter in the Instant Pot and hit Sauté and Adjust so it's on the More or High setting. Once the butter's melted, sear the meat on all sides until lightly browned but not fully cooked, 2–3 minutes. Remove the meat with a slotted spoon and set aside.

CONTINUES

JEFF'S TIP It's important to cook the noodles separately on the stove; pressure cooking will make them mushy, as they'll absorb too much of the sauce.

3 Add the onion to the pot, add the remaining 3 tablespoons of butter, and cook, stirring occasionally, for 2 minutes, until the onion is beginning to soften. Add the mushrooms and cook for 3 minutes more. Add the garlic and cook for another minute.

4 Add the white wine and sauté for a minute, scraping up any browned bits from the bottom of the pan, then add the Dijon mustard and seasoned salt and stir well.

5 Pour in the beef broth, add the thyme, and nestle the beef pieces in the sauce.

6 Secure the lid, move the valve to the sealing position, hit Keep Warm/Cancel followed by Manual or Pressure Cook on High Pressure for 20 minutes. When done, allow a 10-minute natural release followed by a quick release.

7 Meanwhile, stir together the cornstarch with 4 tablespoons cold water to form a slurry. Set aside.

8 When the lid comes off, hit Keep Warm/Cancel and then hit Sauté and Adjust so it's on the More or High setting. Bring the pot to a simmer and immediately stir in the cornstarch slurry. Add the onion soup packet and let bubble for 30 seconds before turning the pot to the Keep Warm setting.

9 Once the bubbles have mostly subsided, stir in the sour cream and Boursin (or cream cheese) until melded.

10 Serve over egg noodles.

MEATLOAF & MASHED POTATOES

This delectable Bundt-style meatloaf lets you make creamy mashed potatoes at the same time and then present it as if it were a Meatloaf & Mashed Potato Cake! It's so game-changing, it was featured on the *Rachael Ray Show*.

Prep Time	Pressure Building Time	Pressure Cook Time	Optional Oven Time	Total Time	Serves
10 minutes	**10–15** minutes	**35** minutes	**5–10** minutes	**75** minutes	**4–6**

THE MEATLOAF

- 2 pounds ground meat (I use a mix of beef, pork, and veal)
- 1 cup breadcrumbs
- ½ cup grated Parmesan cheese
- ½ cup whole milk
- 2 large eggs, lightly beaten
- 9 cloves garlic, minced or pressed
- ½ yellow onion, grated
- 2 tablespoons ketchup
- 2 tablespoons barbecue sauce
- 2 tablespoons dried parsley
- 1 tablespoon seasoned salt
- 2 teaspoons black pepper
- 2 teaspoons dried oregano

THE MASHED POTATOES

- 3 pounds mixed baby white and red potatoes, rinsed, skins on, and quartered
- 1½ cups chicken broth
- 5 cloves of garlic
- 4 tablespoons (½ stick) salted butter
- ½ cup heavy cream or half-and-half
- 1 (5.2-ounce) package Boursin spread (any flavor) or 4 ounces cream cheese, cut into chunky cubes
- 1 teaspoon kosher salt
- 1 teaspoon black pepper
- 1 teaspoon garlic powder
- ½ teaspoon Italian seasoning
- ¼ cup chives, sliced

THE GLAZE

- ½ cup ketchup
- ¼ cup barbecue sauce
- 2 tablespoons brown sugar (light or dark)
- 1 tablespoon yellow mustard
- 1 tablespoon honey
- 1 tablespoon balsamic glaze
- 1 teaspoon Worcestershire sauce

1 In a large bowl, mix together the meatloaf ingredients by hand until they stick together (like a giant meatball).

2 Spray a 6-cup Bundt pan (that will fit in your Instant Pot) with nonstick cooking spray and tightly pack the meatloaf mixture into it. Spray a piece of aluminum foil with nonstick spray and cover the pan, puncturing a hole in the middle of the foil so the steam can escape through the center of the Bundt pan. Set aside.

3 Put the potatoes, chicken broth, and garlic in the Instant Pot. Rest the trivet on top of the potatoes and garlic (press it down so the trivet rests flat; it's okay if you squash some of the potatoes) and then rest the Bundt pan on top of the trivet. Secure the lid, move the valve to the sealing position, and hit Manual or Pressure Cook on High Pressure for 35 minutes. Quick release when done.

4 While the meatloaf's cooking, mix together all the ingredients for the meatloaf glaze in a bowl until well combined; set aside.

5 Carefully remove the Bundt pan from the pot. Pour out any excess drippings from the meatloaf, carefully holding the meatloaf in place with a spatula or towel so it doesn't slide out.

6 *If you wish to caramelize the meatloaf:* Preheat the oven to 400°F. Line a baking sheet with foil coated in nonstick cooking spray. Place the foil-lined baking sheet over the Bundt pan and, firmly holding the pan and foil together with oven mitts, quickly flip the meatloaf out onto the foil. If it breaks apart a little, you can easily push it back into shape. Brush the meatloaf glaze all over the meatloaf and pop it into the oven for 5–10 minutes until the glaze caramelizes. Keep an eye on it as ovens vary!

CONTINUES

JEFF'S TIPS

This recipe makes very smooth and creamy mashed potatoes (which I love). If you want them thicker, use only 1 cup of chicken broth.

If you want to make the meatloaf without the potatoes, in Step 3 just rest the Bundt on the trivet and add 1½ cups of water instead of chicken broth.

7 Meanwhile, use a potato masher to mash the potatoes to the desired consistency and stir in the butter, cream, Boursin (or cream cheese), kosher salt, black pepper, garlic powder, Italian seasoning, and chives.

8 Remove the meatloaf from the Bundt pan (or the oven if you caramelized it) and carefully transfer to a serving dish. Brush with the meatloaf glaze. Place some of the mashed potatoes in the center of the ring (for presentation) and place the rest in a serving dish.

CORNED BEEF
& CABBAGE

This show-stopping Corned Beef & Cabbage is hearty, completely irresistible, and has a beer-based au jus that is simply to-die-for delicious.

Prep Time	Pressure Building Time	Pressure Cook Time	Natural Release Time	Total Time	Serves
5 minutes	10–20 minutes	73 minutes	15 minutes	2 hours	4–6

- **1 medium yellow onion, cut into quarters**
- **3 cloves garlic, minced or pressed**
- **2–4-pound corned beef brisket, with spice/seasoning pack included in the packaging**
- **12 ounces Guinness or beef broth**
- **1 pound Idaho or russet potatoes, peeled and cut into 1-inch cubes**
- **4 large carrots, peeled and cut into 1½-inch lengths**
- **1 head of cabbage, hard bottom removed and cut into 6 wedges**

1 Insert the trivet into the Instant Pot, handles facing up. Place the onion and garlic on the trivet.

2 Remove the corned beef brisket from the package, reserve the spice packet, and rinse the meat thoroughly under cool water to wash off the salty brine.

3 Place the corned beef on top of the onion and garlic, fat side up. Sprinkle the contents of the seasoning packet evenly on top of the brisket and around it in the pot. Pour in the beer, carefully, so as not to wash away the spices from the brisket.

CONTINUES

4 Secure the lid, move the valve to the sealing position, and hit Manual or Pressure Cook on High Pressure for 70 minutes. When done, allow a 15-minute natural release, followed by a quick release.

5 Remove the trivet and transfer just the corned beef to a casserole dish. Reserve 2 cups of the liquid separately, leaving the rest in the pot. Using a paper towel or clean hands, brush the seasonings off the brisket (they will be more difficult to remove when it has cooled) and discard.

6 Add the potatoes, carrots, and cabbage to the Instant Pot. Don't worry if it seems like a tight fit—it'll be fine.

7 Secure the lid, move the valve to the sealing position, hit Keep Warm/Cancel, and then hit Manual or Pressure Cook on High Pressure for 3 minutes.

8 Meanwhile, slice the corned beef against the grain (meaning the opposite direction that the strings of meat are going in).

9 Take the 2 cups of reserved broth and pour it over the brisket in the casserole dish. Cover with aluminum foil.

10 When the veggies are done, perform a quick release and transfer the vegetables to the casserole dish. Any additional broth in the pot may be spooned over the meat to keep it moist and extra flavorful before serving.

 JEFF'S TIPS If you want the carrots and potatoes firmer, wrap them in foil and place on top of the corned beef before pressure cooking.

If cooking more than 4 pounds of corned beef, add 5–10 minutes of cooking time for each additional pound.

ORANGE SESAME BEEF

Whether I'm in a Chinese restaurant or at an airport food court scarfing it down between connecting flights, I can never resist Orange Sesame Beef. But then again, who can? This simple family favorite goes great over Hibachi Fried Rice (page 108) and always yields lots of compliments for the cook!

Prep Time	Sauté Time	Pressure Building Time	Pressure Cook Time	Natural Release Time	Total Time	Serves
5 minutes	10 minutes	10–15 minutes	12 minutes	10 Minutes	50 minutes	4–6

- **2** tablespoons sesame oil
- **1** medium yellow onion, diced
- **3** cloves garlic, minced
- **2–3** pounds flank steak, sliced into ¼-inch strips

- **¾** cup orange juice
- **¾** cup beef broth
- **½** cup light- or dark-brown sugar
- **¼** cup low-sodium soy sauce
- **3** tablespoons cornstarch

- **½** cup honey
- **2** tablespoons hoisin sauce
- **1½** tablespoons orange zest
  Sesame seeds, for serving
  Scallions, sliced, for serving

1 Place the sesame oil in the Instant Pot and press Sauté and Adjust to the More or High setting. Heat the oil for 3 minutes, then add the onion and sauté, stirring, for 3 minutes, until softened. Add the garlic and sauté for 1 minute more.

2 Add the beef and sauté until lightly seared on all sides, about 2 minutes.

3 Add the orange juice, beef broth, brown sugar, and soy sauce and stir to combine. Secure the lid, move the valve to the sealing position, hit Keep Warm/Cancel and then Pressure Cook or Manual on High Pressure for 12 minutes. When done, allow a 10-minute natural release followed by a quick release.

4 Meanwhile, make a cornstarch slurry by mixing the cornstarch with 3 tablespoons cold water. Set aside.

5 Stir in the honey and hoisin sauce. Press Keep Warm/Cancel, and then Sauté and Adjust so it's on the More or High setting and bring the sauce to a simmer. Once the sauce is simmering, immediately stir in the cornstarch slurry and zest and allow to simmer for 30 seconds before turning the pot to the Keep Warm setting.

6 Serve topped with sesame seeds and/or scallions.

 JEFF'S TIP If you'd rather make this with chicken instead of beef, simply substitute 2 pounds boneless, skinless chicken breasts cut into bite-size pieces or tenderloins cut into ¼-inch strips, and reduce the pressure cooking time to 5 minutes.

PULLED PORK

If you've ever wanted to just throw a hunk of meat in your Instant Pot and end up with tasty, lip-smackin' barbecue pulled pork, meet your new favorite recipe.

Prep Time	Pressure Building Time	Pressure Cook Time	Natural Release Time	Total Time	Serves
5 minutes	**10–15** minutes	**60** minutes	**10** minutes	**90** minutes	**4–6**

- 1 tablespoon light- or dark-brown sugar
- 1 tablespoon onion powder
- 1 tablespoon garlic powder
- 1½ teaspoons paprika
- 1½ teaspoons ground cumin

- 1 teaspoon salt
- 1 teaspoon black pepper
- 3–4-pound boneless pork shoulder or butt, cut into 1-pound segments (you can also use country-style ribs)
- 1 tablespoon liquid smoke

- 1 large Spanish (or yellow) onion, quartered
- 2 cups Coca-Cola or Dr Pepper
- 1 cup barbecue sauce (use your favorite)
- Potato rolls or hamburger buns, for serving

1 In a large bowl, mix together the sugar, onion powder, garlic powder, paprika, cumin, salt, and pepper.

2 Brush the pork with the liquid smoke and then roll in the bowl with the spices to coat. Set aside.

 JEFF'S TIP If you like your pork spicy, feel free to add some sriracha, chili powder, or Cajun/Creole seasoning. Or make it Hawaiian style with a mango barbecue sauce!

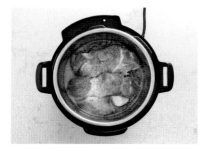

3 Place the onion wedges in the Instant Pot, round sides down. Add the soda and lay the pork pieces on top of the onion.

4 Secure the lid, move the valve to the sealing position, and hit Manual or Pressure Cook on High Pressure for 60 minutes. When done, allow a 10-minute natural release, followed by a quick release.

5 Transfer the pork and onion to a mixing bowl. Reserve ¼ cup of the juices from the pot and discard the rest.

6 Shred the pork and onion with a pair of forks or a hand mixer, and mix in the reserved juices and barbecue sauce before serving with some slaw in rolls or buns.

SWEDISH
MEATBALLS

There's a certain Swedish furniture store I sometimes visit— not to look at furniture, but to eat the meatballs in their cafeteria. My Swedish Meatballs are delicious on their own, but once they go for a swim in a delightfully creamy sauce, you just may find yourself pouring it over rice and egg noodles.

Prep Time	Sauté Time	Pressure Building Time	Pressure Cook Time	Natural Release Time	Total Time	Serves
5 minutes	5 minutes	10–15 minutes	10 minutes	5 minutes	40 minutes	4–6

THE MEATBALLS

- **1 pound ground beef (the less lean, the better)**
- **½ pound ground pork**
- **⅓ cup whole milk**
- **⅓ cup plain breadcrumbs**
- **1 large egg, lightly beaten**
- **3 cloves garlic, minced**
- **2 tablespoons dried parsley flakes**
- **1½ teaspoons seasoned salt**
- **1½ teaspoons onion powder**
- **½ teaspoon white pepper**
- **¼ teaspoon black pepper**
- **¼ teaspoon allspice**
- **2 cups beef broth**

THE SAUCE

- **2 tablespoons cornstarch**
- **5 tablespoons salted butter**
- **½ cup heavy cream**
- **1 packet beef gravy mix**
- **1 teaspoon Dijon mustard**

1 Make the meatballs: With clean hands, mix all of the ingredients (except for the broth) in a large mixing bowl. Form about 24 meatballs, each about the size of a Ping-Pong ball.

2 Add the trivet to the pot. Pour the broth in the pot and add the meatballs, carefully allowing them to rest on top of one another. Secure the lid, move the valve to the sealing position, and hit Manual or Pressure Cook on High Pressure for 10 minutes. When done, allow a 5-minute natural release followed by a quick release.

3 Transfer the meatballs to a plate and set aside. Remove the trivet, leaving the broth in the Instant Pot. Meanwhile, mix the cornstarch with 2 tablespoons cold water and set aside.

4 Press Keep Warm/Cancel, then Sauté and Adjust so it's on the More or High setting. Stir in the butter, cream, gravy mix, and mustard and bring to a simmer. Once the sauce bubbles, immediately stir in the cornstarch slurry. Allow to simmer for 10 seconds and then turn the pot off.

5 Add the meatballs back to the pot, stir to coat in the sauce, and serve.

 JEFF'S TIPS **Want it keto?** Leave out the breadcrumbs (although the meatballs will be slightly looser) and use a keto-friendly gravy mix.

If you wish to use frozen meatballs, go for it. Skip all the meatball ingredients and **Step 1**. Pressure cook time remains the same.

SPICED SHORT RIBS

Don't be fooled by short ribs. They aren't short in flavor and they aren't like the ribs you may be thinking of. This cut of meat is one of the most succulent available, and when we pair it with a festive-inspired wine-based sauce? All bets are off.

Prep Time	Sauté Time	Pressure Building Time	Pressure Cook Time	Natural Release Time	Total Time	Serves
5 minutes	10 minutes	10–20 minutes	45 minutes	15 minutes	90 minutes	4–6

1 cup beef broth

¾ cup dry red wine (like a cabernet)

½ cup hoisin sauce

3 cloves garlic, minced or pressed

1 teaspoon ground allspice

1 teaspoon cinnamon

1 teaspoon Chinese five spice powder (optional)

5–6 pounds bone-in short ribs

Kosher salt and black pepper, to season ribs (about 1½ teaspoons of each)

1 large Spanish (or yellow) onion, quartered

¼ cup cornstarch

½ cup honey

1 Create the sauce by whisking together the beef broth, red wine, hoisin sauce, garlic, allspice, cinnamon, and five spice powder (if using). Set aside.

2 Lightly rub the short ribs all over with kosher salt and black pepper.

3 Hit Sauté and Adjust so it's on the More or High setting. After 2 minutes of heating, working in batches, sear the short ribs for 1 minute on each side and set aside.

4 Add about ½ cup of the sauce to the pot and stir, scraping up any browned bits from the bottom. Once the bottom is clear, hit Keep Warm/Cancel to turn the pot off.

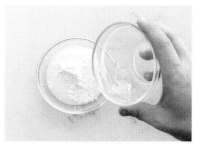

5 Add the onion wedges, rounded side down, then rest all the short ribs on top of the onion and pour the remaining sauce on top.

6 Secure the lid, move the valve to the sealing position, hit Keep Warm/Cancel, and then hit Manual or Pressure Cook on High Pressure for 45 minutes. Allow a 15-minute natural release when done, followed by a quick release.

7 Meanwhile, combine the cornstarch with ¼ cup cold water to form a slurry and set aside.

8 Carefully remove the ribs from the pot (they will be tender and prone to falling apart) and place in a serving dish. Hit Keep Warm/Cancel followed by Sauté and Adjust so it's on the High or More setting and bring the sauce to a bubble. Add the honey and the cornstarch slurry, stirring immediately. Let simmer for 30 seconds before hitting Keep Warm/Cancel to turn the pot off. Let stand 5 minutes.

9 Pour the sauce over the short ribs and serve with some bread to sop up the extra sauce.

JEFF'S TIP

For a wonderful side dish, try my **Cauliflower Puree (page 246).**

SAUSAGE & PEPPERS
PARMESAN

If you haven't noticed by now, I love putting my own spin on classic dishes. Here, we take simple sausage and peppers and elevate them with a Parmesan cream broth. This is perfect on its own, in a hero, or served over rice or pasta.

Prep Time	Sauté Time	Pressure Building Time	Pressure Cook Time	Total Time	Serves
5 minutes	18 minutes	10–20 minutes	5 minutes	45 minutes	4–6

- 3 tablespoons extra-virgin olive oil
- 2 tablespoons (¼ stick) salted butter
- 2 Vidalia (sweet) onions, cut into strands
- 2 green bell peppers, cut lengthwise into slices

- 2 red bell peppers, cut lengthwise into slices
- 6 cloves garlic, minced or pressed
- 2 pounds Italian sausage links (sweet and/or hot), sliced into disks ½ inch thick
- ½ cup dry white wine (like a chardonnay)

- 1 teaspoon oregano
- 1 teaspoon Italian seasoning
- 1 cup grated Parmesan cheese
- 1 (5.2-ounce) package Boursin spread (any flavor) or 4 ounces cream cheese, cut into chunky cubes

1 Place the olive oil and butter in the Instant Pot and hit Sauté and Adjust so it's on the More or High setting. Once the butter's melted, add the onion and peppers. Sauté for 10 minutes, until softened and the onion is beginning to brown. Add the garlic and cook for 1 minute more.

2 Add the sausage and cook for 2–3 minutes until lightly browned. Don't worry that the insides are still raw—that changes when it's pressure cooked.

3 Add in the wine, followed by the oregano and Italian seasoning, and sauté for another 1–2 minutes, until simmering and fragrant.

4 Secure the lid, move the valve to the sealing position, hit the Keep Warm/Cancel button, and then hit Manual or Pressure Cook on High Pressure for 5 minutes. Quick release when done.

5 Stir in the Parmesan and Boursin (or cream cheese) until melted and creamy.

6 Serve with crusty bread to mop up the sauce, over White or Brown Rice (page 26) or pasta or as a hero (see below).

 JEFF'S TIPS

To make a sausage Parmesan hero, slice a Portuguese or hero roll down the top (like a split-top hot dog bun, used in my Lobster Rolls, page 212) and use a slotted spoon to add the sausage and veggies. Cover the top with a few slices of mozzarella or other cheese, place on a foil-lined baking sheet, and broil for 1½–2 minutes on high on the top rack of your oven—or on the trivet in the Instant Pot Duo Crisp on Broil at 400°F for 1–3 minutes—until the cheese is browned and bubbling.

A great way to slice raw sausage links easily is to pop them in the freezer for 5 minutes before slicing. They hold their form much better this way!

DIJON DILL PORK TENDERLOIN

These plump and juicy medallions of pork tenderloin are irresistible when draped with this creamy Dijon mustard sauce (just don't tell my rabbi). At the market, be sure you buy pork tenderloin, not pork loin—that's a totally different cut of meat.

Prep Time	Sauté Time	Pressure Building Time	Pressure Cook Time	Natural Release Time	Total Time	Serves
5 minutes	2 minutes	10–15 minutes	8 minutes	10 minutes	40 minutes	4–6

2   pounds pork tenderloin

2   cups chicken broth

½   cup Dijon mustard, divided

4   tablespoons (½ stick) salted butter

4   tablespoons cornstarch

Juice of 1 lemon

½   cup fresh dill, chopped, plus more for garnish

1 Slice the pork into medallions or disks about 1 inch thick.

2 Pour the broth and ¼ cup of the mustard into the Instant Pot and stir to combine. Add the pork and top off with the butter.

3 Secure the lid, move the valve to the sealing position, and hit Manual or Pressure Cook on High Pressure for 8 minutes. When done, allow a 10-minute natural release and follow with a quick release.

4 Meanwhile, mix together the cornstarch and 4 tablespoons cold water to form a slurry.

5 When the pot has finished cooking, transfer the pork to a serving dish and set aside.

6 On the Instant Pot, hit Keep Warm/Cancel and then Sauté and Adjust so it's on the More or High setting. Stir in the lemon juice and the remaining ¼ cup of mustard and bring to a simmer.

7 Once bubbling, immediately stir in the cornstarch slurry and let simmer until beginning to thicken, about a minute. Hit Keep Warm/Cancel to turn the pot off and let stand until thickened to your liking, about 5 minutes.

8 Stir in the dill and pour the sauce over the pork to serve, then garnish with more dill.

JEFF'S TIP

This recipe goes great with **White or Brown Rice (page 26)**, noodles or zoodles, or other veggies.

HUNGARIAN GOULASH

What can be more comforting than a bowl of melt-in-your-mouth beef in a grand and delightfully lush sauce served over a bed of fluffy egg noodles? (That was a rhetorical question.)

Prep Time	Sauté Time	Pressure Building Time	Pressure Cook Time	Natural Release Time	Total Time	Serves
5 minutes	10 minutes	15–20 minutes	30 minutes	10 minutes	75 minutes	4–6

- 4 tablespoons (½ stick) salted butter, divided
- 1 large Spanish (or yellow) onion, cut lengthwise into thin slices
- 2 tablespoons paprika
- 1 teaspoon caraway seeds
- 3 pounds beef stew meat or chuck cubes

- ½ cup dry red wine (like a pinot noir)
- 1½ cups beef broth
- 2 cups baby carrots
- 1 (14.5-ounce) can diced tomatoes
- ¼ cup ketchup
- 3 tablespoons dark-brown sugar

- 1 tablespoon white vinegar
- 1 tablespoon seasoned salt
- 1 teaspoon black pepper
- 3 tablespoons cornstarch
- 1 (12-ounce) package egg noodles, prepared separately, cooked according to package directions

1 Place 2 tablespoons of butter in the Instant Pot. Hit Sauté and Adjust so it's on the More or High setting. Once the butter's melted, add the onion and sauté for 3 minutes, until beginning to soften.

2 Add the paprika, caraway seeds, and remaining 2 tablespoons of butter, stirring constantly so the paprika doesn't stick to the bottom of the pot.

3 Add the meat and sauté for 2–3 minutes, stirring constantly, until it is lightly seared but not fully cooked.

4 Add the wine and deglaze the bottom of the pot for 1 minute, scraping any brown bits that may have gotten stuck on. Add the remaining ingredients except for the cornstarch and egg noodles and stir to combine.

5 Secure the lid, move the valve to the sealing position, and hit Keep Warm/Cancel, then Manual or Pressure Cook on High for 30 minutes. When done, allow a 10-minute natural release followed by a quick release.

6 Meanwhile, mix the cornstarch with 3 tablespoons cold water to form a slurry. Set aside.

7 Once the lid's off, hit Keep Warm/Cancel and then Sauté and Adjust so it's on the More or High setting. Once the sauce comes to a bubble, immediately stir in the cornstarch slurry and let simmer for a minute, until thickened.

8 Serve over egg noodles.

  This also works well as a fancy Sloppy Joe. Swap the egg noodles for buns of your choice!

SHEPHERD'S PIE

When I was growing up, this was one of my favorite meals. Perfect for hearty appetites, this "pie" has no crust—just a layer of juicy meat richly simmered and topped off with creamy mashed potatoes. It's absolutely perfect for when the weather's brisk, and it's a great reward for shoveling the driveway.

Prep Time	Sauté Time	Pressure Building Time	Pressure Cook Time	Total Time	Serves
5 minutes	**10** minutes	**10–15** minutes	**12** minutes	**45** minutes	**4–6**

THE MEAT

- ¼ cup extra-virgin olive oil
- 1 large yellow onion, diced
- 3 cloves garlic, minced
- 1½ pounds ground meat (I like ground lamb or a veal, pork, and beef mix)
- ½ cup dry red wine (like a cabernet)
- 1 teaspoon seasoned salt
- 1 teaspoon Italian seasoning
- ¼ teaspoon nutmeg
- 1 (10-ounce) box frozen mixed peas and carrots
- 4 tablespoons tomato paste, divided

THE POTATOES

- 1½ pounds baby potatoes (any color you like), skin on
- 3 tablespoons salted butter
- ¼ cup heavy cream or half-and-half
- Half package (3 ounces) of Boursin spread (any flavor) or 2 ounces cream cheese, cut into chunky cubes
- ½ teaspoon garlic salt
- 1 teaspoon black pepper

1 On the Instant Pot, hit Sauté and Adjust to the More or High setting. Pour in the oil and heat for 3 minutes, then add the onion and sauté until softened, about 3 minutes. Add the garlic and sauté for 1 minute more.

2 Add the beef and sauté for 2 minutes, until beginning to brown, and then add the wine, seasoned salt, Italian seasoning, and nutmeg and bring to a simmer, scraping up any browned bits from the bottom of the pot. Add in the peas and carrots and stir in 2 tablespoons of the tomato paste, then cook for 1 minute longer.

3 Using a mixing spoon, scoop the meat mixture into a round 1½-quart oven-safe casserole dish that will fit in your Instant Pot.

4 Pour 1 cup of water into the Instant Pot and scrape the bottom so any remnants of meat come up. Don't pour the water out—it's needed to build pressure. Place the trivet in the pot and rest the casserole dish on top. Top the meat with the whole baby potatoes.

5 Secure the lid, hit Keep Warm/Cancel, and then hit Pressure Cook or Manual on High Pressure for 12 minutes. Quick release when done.

6 Carefully move the potatoes to a bowl and mash them to the desired consistency. Mix in the butter, cream, Boursin (or cream cheese), garlic salt, and black pepper.

7 Using oven mitts, carefully remove the casserole dish from the trivet and Instant Pot. Skim off excess juices by pressing the back of a mixing spoon against the top of the meat and letting the spoon fill; discard. About 5 spoonfuls should do the trick. Stir in the remaining 2 tablespoons of tomato paste, layer the mashed potatoes on top, and serve.

JEFF'S TIPS Want a lovely crusted top to the potatoes? Fancy! Just before serving, preheat the oven to broil and pop in the assembled Shepherd's Pie for 2–5 minutes (keep an eye on it as ovens vary).

Want it keto? Sub a head of cauliflower for the potatoes and reduce the pressure cooking time to 3 minutes.

Any juices at the bottom of the dish are great to drizzle over the meat and potatoes while serving.

SEAFOOD

If you're a seafood lover, you've just met your match. Just toss fish, shrimp, lobster, crab, and mussels into the pot and go. These delicious recipes will put the ocean in motion.

Shrimp Boil
208

Mussels in White
Wine Sauce
210

Lobster Rolls
212

Seafood Fra
Diavolo
214

Sweet & Sassy
Shrimp
216

Lemon Pepper
Miso–Glazed
Salmon
218

Tropical Tilapia
220

Coconut Curry
Mahi Mahi
222

SHRIMP BOIL

This is truly the fanciest "dump & go" recipe ever. Not only is it loaded with shrimp, sausage, corn, and potatoes, but it's astounding how the flavors achieve a crustacean crescendo in this unforgettable Shrimp Boil.

Prep Time	Pressure Building Time	Pressure Cook Time	Total Time	Serves
5 minutes	35 minutes	0 minutes	40 minutes	4–6

3 large red potatoes, skins on, quartered

1 Vidalia (sweet) onion, cut in chunks

6 frozen (or fresh) corn-on-the-cob halves

1 (12-ounce) package precooked smoked sausage of your choice, cut into about ½-inch slices (I used chicken jalapeño sausage; andouille also works)

2 pounds large uncooked frozen shrimp (unpeeled)

1 tablespoon Old Bay seasoning

1 teaspoon crushed red pepper (optional)

1 teaspoon Zatarain's Crab & Shrimp Boil concentrate (optional; omit if you don't want spice)

½ teaspoon seasoned salt

½ teaspoon black pepper

9 cloves garlic, minced or pressed

1 cup chicken broth

1 Place all ingredients in the Instant Pot in this order: potatoes and onions on the bottom, followed by the corn resting on top and arranged in a ring against the perimeter of the pot, followed by the sausage in the middle of the corn ring, and topped with the shrimp. Finish by adding the seasonings, garlic and broth.

2 Secure the lid, move the valve to the sealing position, and hit Manual or Pressure Cook on High Pressure for 0 (yes, *zero*) minutes. Quick release when done.

3 Serve with some delicious crusty bread for dipping into the broth.

JEFF'S TIP

Since we have frozen corn cobs and frozen shrimp in the pot, this will likely take 35 minutes just to come to pressure. And it may not even come to pressure and will just turn to the L0:00 or 00:00 setting after 35 minutes—which is totally fine! If that happens, and the pin never goes up, just open the lid without a need for a Quick Release. It will be fully cooked!

MUSSELS

IN WHITE WINE SAUCE

It's time to flex your mussels. Actually, you don't even have to since this dish is easier (and tastier) than working out. This dish pairs perfectly with garlic bread or French fries.

Prep Time	Sauté Time	Pressure Building Time	Pressure Cook Time	Total Time	Serves
5 minutes	5 minutes	10–15 minutes	3 minutes	25 minutes	4–6

- **6 tablespoons (¾ stick) salted butter**
- **4 shallots, minced**
- **9 cloves garlic, minced or pressed**

- **¾ cup dry white wine (like a sauvignon blanc)**
- **3 tablespoons parsley flakes**
- **3–5 pounds fresh mussels, rinsed and debearded (make sure to toss out any that have already opened before cooking)**

- **1½ cups chicken broth or garlic broth (e.g. Garlic Better Than Bouillon)**
- **Juice of 3 lemons**
- **A fresh, crusty baguette, for serving**

1 Place the butter in the Instant Pot, then hit Sauté and Adjust so it's on the More or High setting. Once the butter's melted, add the shallots and cook for about 2 minutes until beginning to brown, then add the garlic and sauté for 1 minute more.

2 Add the wine and stir, scraping up any browned bits from the bottom of the pot. Let simmer 1–2 minutes, until slightly thickened.

3 Stir in the parsley and add the mussels (you can fill the pot to the brim so long as there's room for the lid) and pour the broth and lemon juice over everything.

JEFF'S TIPS

You can use half the mussels and the pressure cook time will remain the same.

If any mussels haven't opened after cooking, toss them.

4 Secure the lid, move the valve to the sealing position, hit Keep Warm/Cancel and then hit Manual or Pressure Cook on High Pressure for 3 minutes. Quick release when done.

5 Serve immediately, sopping up any juices with the crusty baguette.

LOBSTER
ROLLS

I'm a sucker for the perfect lobster roll. Now, the definition of "perfect" can cause a full-on war in New England—some like theirs draped with melted butter and others prefer a creamy dressing. I go for the best of both worlds with a melted butter–based dressing that will have everyone sitting on the dock toasting these masterpieces.

Prep Time	Pressure Building Time	Pressure Cook Time	Total Time	Serves
10	**5–10**	**4**	**30**	**4**
minutes	minutes	minutes	(45 minutes with refrigeration time)	

- 1½ cups water
- 1 teaspoon Old Bay seasoning (plus a few shakes for the broth)
- 2 pounds fresh warm- or cold-water lobster tails, in shell
  Juice of 1 lemon, divided

- 2–3 scallions, thinly sliced
- ½ cup mayonnaise
- 4 tablespoons (½ stick) unsalted butter, melted, divided
- ⅛ teaspoon celery salt
  Hot dog buns (preferably top-sliced ones), for serving

JEFF'S TIP Not into lobster rolls but just want to eat the lobster tails dipped in melted butter? *Go for it!* You're done after Step 3—just leave the tail intact once you remove it from the shell.

1 Pour the water into the Instant Pot with a few sprinkles of Old Bay seasoning. Add the trivet and lay each lobster tail, shell side down, on the trivet. Squeeze half the lemon over the lobster.

2 Secure the lid, move the valve to the sealing position, and hit Manual or Pressure Cook on High Pressure for 4 minutes (adjust cook time to 3 minutes for less than 2 pounds of lobster, and to 5 minutes for 3–4 pounds). Quick release when done and immediately transfer the lobsters to an ice bath to stop the cooking.

3 Once cooled, place the lobster tails curved shell down on a cutting board and use kitchen shears to cut the hard shell of the tail down the center. Remove the meat from the shell and chop it up into bite-size chunks.

4 In a mixing bowl, add the lobster meat, scallions, mayo, 2 tablespoons of the melted butter, celery salt, Old Bay, and the juice of the remaining lemon half. Mix well and transfer to the fridge for at least 15 minutes, or a few hours, to cool and set.

5 When you're ready to serve, brush the buns with the remaining 2 tablespoons of melted butter. Lay the buns butter side down in a preheated frying pan over medium heat and press with a spatula for about 2 minutes until lightly browned.

6 Fill each roll with lobster meat and enjoy!

SEAFOOD
FRA DIAVOLO

"Fra Diavolo" sounds like something a bit mischievous and mysterious. It's actually just an irresistibly spicy tomato-based sauce that tastes great in this seafood pasta.

Prep Time	Sauté Time	Pressure Building Time	Pressure Cook Time	Total Time	Serves
5 minutes	**8** minutes	**5–10** minutes	**12** minutes	**35** minutes	**4–6**

3　tablespoons extra-virgin olive oil

4　tablespoons (½ stick) salted butter

1　pound langostino meat

2　shallots, diced

10　cloves garlic, thinly sliced

3　cups Marinara Sauce (page 34; but look for the Victoria brand if you don't feel like making your own), divided

3　cups fish broth (e.g. Fish Better Than Bouillon) or chicken broth

½　cup hot sauce

8–10　ounces grape or cherry tomatoes

1　teaspoon Italian seasoning

1　teaspoon Old Bay seasoning

1　teaspoon cayenne pepper (optional)

½　teaspoon crushed red pepper flakes (optional)

⅛　teaspoon Zatarain's Concentrated Shrimp & Crab Boil (optional; use up to ½ teaspoon if you like it extra spicy!)

1　pound bucatini (thick, hollow spaghetti)

1　pound lump crabmeat or 3 (6-ounce) cans white or pink crabmeat, drained

　Grated Parmesan cheese, for serving

1 Place the oil and butter in the Instant Pot. Hit Sauté and Adjust so it's on the More or High setting. Once the butter's melted and sizzling, sear the langostino meat for about 2 minutes, being careful not to overcook it. Remove with a slotted spoon and set aside.

2 Add the shallots and garlic and cook for 5 minutes, until lightly browned.

3 Add 1½ cups of the marinara sauce, the broth, hot sauce, cherry tomatoes, Italian seasoning, Old Bay, cayenne (if using), crushed red pepper flakes (if using), and Zatarain's (if using) and stir well, making sure nothing is stuck to the bottom of the pot.

4 Add the pasta by breaking it in half so it fits in the pot but *do not stir*. Just use a mixing spoon to submerge as much of it in the liquid as possible (it's okay if some of the pasta sticks out).

5 Secure the lid, move the valve to the sealing position, hit Keep Warm/Cancel, and then hit Manual or Pressure Cook on High Pressure for 12 minutes. Quick release when done.

6 Add the remaining 1½ cups of marinara sauce and stir everything together, then stir in the reserved langostino and the crabmeat. Let stand, stirring occasionally, for about 2 minutes, until the crab is warm. Serve sprinkled with Parmesan.

 JEFF'S TIPS

Adding the crabmeat after pressure cooking ensures that we don't end up with overcooked, drab crab.

Want to include some shrimp or calamari? Add about 1 pound of raw shrimp or calamari (or a mix of both) with the crabmeat in Step 6 and toss with the pasta. The residual heat will cook it within a few minutes—you'll know it's done when the shrimp is pink and opaque and the tails curl up.

Want to make this amazing fra diavolo without the seafood? Leave out the langostino and crabmeat. Everything else remains the same.

Give it a creamy flair by adding in a 5.2-ounce package of Boursin spread (any flavor) in Step 6.

SWEET & SASSY SHRIMP

I like my food how I like a fun friend: sweet & sassy. This delicious Asian-inspired shrimp dish is coated with a sweet-and-spicy sauce that's totally customizable to your preferred spice level.

Prep Time	Sauté Time	Pressure Building Time	Pressure Cook Time	Total Time	Serves
5 minutes	3 minutes	5–10 minutes	0 minutes	20 minutes	4–6

- 2 pounds jumbo shrimp, tails on or off, peeled and deveined
- 1 tablespoon Cajun or Creole seasoning
- 1 cup garlic broth (e.g. Garlic Better Than Bouillon) or chicken broth
- 1 cup hot sauce (I like Frank's RedHot)
- 1½ cups packed light-brown sugar
- ¼ cup apple cider vinegar
- 3 cloves garlic, minced or pressed
- ½ teaspoon crushed red pepper flakes (more if you want it very spicy!)
- ½ cup honey
- 3 tablespoons cornstarch
- Sesame seeds, for serving (optional)

1 Lightly sprinkle and toss each shrimp with the Cajun or Creole seasoning.

2 On the Instant Pot, hit Sauté and Adjust so it's on the More or High setting. Pour in the broth, hot sauce, brown sugar, vinegar, garlic, and red pepper flakes. Whisk and bring to a boil, then hit Keep Warm/Cancel.

3 Add the shrimp to the pot, secure the lid, move the valve to the sealing position, and hit Manual or Pressure Cook on High Pressure for 0 minutes (yes, *zero* minutes). Quick release when done.

4 Transfer the shrimp to a serving dish to rest and stir the honey into the pot.

5 Stir together the cornstarch with 3 tablespoons cold water to form a slurry. Set aside.

6 Hit the Keep Warm/Cancel button, then hit Sauté and Adjust so it's on the More or High setting. Once the sauce bubbles, immediately stir in the cornstarch slurry and let bubble for 30 seconds before hitting Keep Warm/Cancel again. The sauce should be thick enough to cling to the shrimp.

7 Pour the sauce over the shrimp, sprinkle with sesame seeds, if desired, and serve immediately. This dish goes great with my Hibachi Fried Rice (page 108).

JEFF'S TIPS If you're using frozen shrimp, no need to thaw them first—just set the cook time to 1 minute instead of zero minutes. This will make your shrimp more well-done.

If you'd rather just use your Instant Pot to sauté your shrimp, go for it! It's a great way to use the Instant Pot as a stovetop pot, without the stove. Simply add the shrimp to the other ingredients in Step 2 and keep the setting on Sauté on More or High for 3 minutes or so until cooked through (shrimp should look totally pink and opaque). Skip Step 3 and then continue with the recipe.

LEMON PEPPER
MISO-GLAZED
SALMON

When I was an inexperienced cook, the very thought of cooking fish intimidated me. Once I finally got up the courage to try salmon in the Instant Pot, I was a total convert. It turns out this salmon dish is one of the easiest things you'll ever make—and its sweet and savory sauce will make you feel like a pro.

Prep Time	Sauté Time	Pressure Building Time	Pressure Cook Time	Total Time	Serves
5 minutes	**3** minutes	**5–10** minutes	**4** minutes	**25** minutes	**4–6**

- **4–6 salmon fillets, skin on or off, cut about 1 inch thick**
- **1 tablespoon lemon pepper seasoning**
- **1 cup vegetable broth**
- **¼ cup dark-brown sugar**

- **2 tablespoons sesame oil**
- **2 tablespoons low-sodium soy sauce**
- **2 tablespoons fish sauce**
- **Juice of 1 lemon**

- **2 tablespoons white miso paste (though any kind will work)**
- **1 tablespoon cornstarch**
- **Sliced scallions, for serving**
- **Sesame seeds, for serving**

1 Lightly rub the salmon fillets with the lemon pepper seasoning. Set aside.

2 Put the broth, sugar, sesame oil, soy sauce, fish sauce, lemon juice, and miso paste in the Instant Pot and whisk until the sugar has dissolved into the sauce.

3 Place a parchment round on the trivet. Lay the salmon on the parchment round (it's okay if the fillets rest on each other) and use the handles to lower the trivet into the pot.

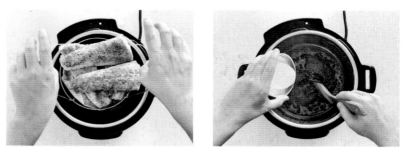

4 Secure the lid, move the valve to the sealing position, and hit Manual or Pressure Cook on High Pressure for 4 minutes. Quick release when done.

5 Stir together the cornstarch with 1 tablespoon cold water to form a slurry. Set aside.

6 Carefully remove the trivet with the salmon and rest on a plate. Hit Keep Warm/Cancel and then hit Sauté and Adjust so it's on More or High. Once bubbling, immediately stir in the slurry and hit Keep Warm/Cancel to turn the pot off.

7 Spoon some sauce over the salmon, garnish with sliced scallions and sesame seeds, and serve with White or Brown Rice (page 26) or Crabby Creamed Corn (page 248).

 JEFF'S TIP If you're using frozen salmon, increase the pressure cooking time to 6 minutes.

TROPICAL TILAPIA

Sometimes all it takes is the perfect sauce to make a dish sing. With its sweet and tangy Hawaiian-style sauce, this dish is lightning-quick to make, but the flavor is so wonderfully rich, you'd never know it.

Prep Time	Sauté Time	Pressure Building Time	Pressure Cook Time	Total Time	Serves
5 minutes	3 minutes	5–10 minutes	3 minutes	25 minutes	4–6

2 red bell peppers, diced
1 (16-ounce) bottle Catalina or California French salad dressing

⅔ cup honey
2 tablespoons apple cider vinegar
4–6 tilapia fillets, skin on or off, cut about ½–1-inch thick

2 tablespoons cornstarch
1 (20-ounce) can crushed pineapple, drained

1 In the Instant Pot, add the bell peppers, dressing, honey, and vinegar. Stir well.

2 Place a parchment round on the trivet. Lay the tilapia on the parchment round (it's okay if the fillets rest on each other) and use the handles to lower the trivet into the pot. Brush some of the sauce over the tilapia.

3 Secure the lid, move the valve to the sealing position, and hit Manual or Pressure Cook on High Pressure for 3 minutes. Quick release when done.

4 Meanwhile, mix the cornstarch with 2 tablespoons cold water to form a slurry. Set aside.

5 Carefully remove the trivet and transfer the tilapia to a serving platter. Hit Keep Warm/Cancel and then Sauté so the pot is on the High or More setting and bring to bubbling. Add the cornstarch slurry and immediately stir well, scraping up any settled honey or cornstarch from the bottom of the pan. Bring to a simmer, stirring, then turn the pot off and let the sauce cool and thicken for about 1 minute. Stir in the pineapple.

6 Spoon the sauce over the tilapia and serve with quinoa (page 36), rice, or veggies.

JEFF'S TIP If you're using frozen fish, increase the pressure cooking time to 6 minutes.

COCONUT CURRY MAHI MAHI

This delightfully classic curry sauce has just a hint of sweet and spicy. Here, you'll combine it with mahi mahi, a mild white fish that will complement the flavorful sauce beautifully.

Prep Time	Sauté Time	Pressure Building Time	Pressure Cook Time	Total Time	Serves
5 minutes	**3** minutes	**5–10** minutes	**3** minutes	**25** minutes	**4–6**

- 1 (14-ounce) can unsweetened coconut milk (it should be thin like water and not thick and lumpy)
- 1 tablespoon fish sauce
- Juice of ½ lime
- 1 tablespoon curry powder
- 1 teaspoon granulated sugar
- 1 teaspoon dried thyme
- ½ teaspoon seasoned salt
- ½ teaspoon chili powder (optional)
- 4–6 mahi mahi or tilapia fillets, skin off, cut about 1 inch thick
- ¼ cup fresh tarragon leaves
- 2 tablespoons cornstarch
- ½ cup honey
- ¼ cup heavy cream or half-and-half
- 1 teaspoon balsamic glaze (optional)

1 Whisk together the coconut milk, fish sauce, lime juice, curry powder, sugar, thyme, seasoned salt, and chili powder (if using) in the Instant Pot.

2 Place a parchment round on the trivet. Lay the mahi mahi on the parchment round (it's okay if the fillets rest on each other) and use the handles to lower the trivet into the pot. Brush some of the sauce over the mahi mahi. Sprinkle with the tarragon leaves.

3 Secure the lid, move the valve to the sealing position, and hit Manual or Pressure Cook on High Pressure for 3 minutes. Quick release when done.

4 Meanwhile, mix the cornstarch with 2 tablespoons cold water to form a slurry. Set aside.

5 Carefully remove the trivet and transfer the mahi mahi to a serving platter. Hit Keep Warm/Cancel, then Sauté so the pot is on the High or More setting, and bring the sauce to a simmer. Immediately stir in the cornstarch slurry, scraping up any settled cornstarch from the bottom of the pan. Let it simmer for 30 seconds, stirring, then hit Keep Warm/Cancel to turn the pot off and allow the sauce to thicken.

6 Stir in the honey, cream, and balsamic glaze (if using).

7 Spoon the sauce over the plated mahi mahi. Serve alongside White or Brown Rice (page 26) or Thai Basil Fried Rice (page 124) and veggies of your choice.

JEFF'S TIP If you want the fish more on the rare side, reduce the pressure cooking time to 2 minutes.

VEGETABLES & SIDES

If you're looking for the perfect side dish or a few generous vegetarian mains, this chapter is your North Star. Not only are many of these recipes some of the quickest and easiest in this book, but they are some of the tastiest too!

THE ULTIMATE
BAKED BEANS

The Instant Pot is miraculous at cooking beans. It speeds up the process and requires no babysitting, while keeping your kitchen cool. We dress these gorgeous baked beans to the nines by giving them the smoky flavor of a rustic campfire. Except without the bears and mosquitoes.

Prep Time	Sauté Time	Pressure Building Time	Pressure Cook Time	Natural Release Time	Total Time	Serves
10 minutes	15 minutes	10–20 minutes	25 minutes	25 minutes	90 minutes	4–6

1 **pound dried pinto beans (not canned), rinsed and drained**

8 **cups ham or chicken broth or water (the broth will simply infuse more flavor into the beans)**

2 **tablespoons (¼ stick) salted butter**

1 **pound thick-cut bacon, diced**

1 **large Vidalia (sweet) onion, diced**

1 **tablespoon Worcestershire sauce**

⅓ **cup molasses**

⅓ **cup maple syrup**

⅓ **cup ketchup**

⅓ **cup barbecue sauce**

⅓ **cup dark-brown sugar**

3 **tablespoons tomato paste**

1 **tablespoon Dijon mustard**

2 **teaspoons liquid smoke**

1 **teaspoon ground mustard powder**

¼ **teaspoon allspice (or cinnamon if you don't have allspice in your cupboard)**

1 Place the beans and the broth or water in the Instant Pot. Secure the lid, turn the valve to the sealing position, and hit Manual or Pressure Cook on High Pressure for 25 minutes. When done, allow a 25-minute natural release followed by a quick release. Hit Keep Warm/Cancel to turn the pot off.

2 Carefully remove the liner pot and pour the beans into a colander, rinse with cool water, and set aside. Return the liner pot to the Instant Pot—no need to clean it.

3 Hit Sauté and Adjust so it's on the More or High setting, and add the butter. Once melted, add the bacon and sauté, stirring occasionally, until nice and crispy, about 10 minutes. Set aside the cooked bacon in a paper towel–lined bowl, reserving the bacon grease in the pot.

4 Sauté the onion, stirring occasionally, in the bacon grease for 5 minutes, until beginning to soften. Add the Worcestershire sauce and scrape up any caked-on bacon grease.

5 Add the molasses, maple syrup, ketchup, barbecue sauce, brown sugar, tomato paste, Dijon mustard, liquid smoke, mustard powder, and allspice to the Instant Pot and stir until fully combined. Hit Keep Warm/Cancel and have it stay on the Keep Warm setting.

6 Gently stir the cooked beans and bacon into the sauce, tossing and coating until well combined. Serve with basically any savory dish!

JEFF'S TIPS

Want to keep it vegetarian? Skip the bacon and just cook the onion in the butter.

YELLOW
SPLIT-PEA
CURRY

Inspired by Ethiopian and Indian cuisine, I wanted to play with yellow split peas by transforming them into a quick, creamy, thick, and flavorful vegetarian curry. Mission accomplished.

Prep Time	Sauté Time	Pressure Building Time	Pressure Cook Time	Natural Release Time	Total Time	Serves
5 minutes	7 minutes	5–10 minutes	15 minutes	10 minutes	45 minutes	4–6

- **2 tablespoons (¼ stick) salted butter**
- **1 red onion, diced**
- **6 cloves garlic, minced or pressed**
- **1 tablespoon minced or pressed ginger**

- **2 (14-ounce) cans unsweetened coconut milk (it should be thin like water and not thick and lumpy)**
- **½ cup vegetable broth, plus more if desired after cooking**
- **2 cups yellow split peas or yellow lentils, rinsed**
- **2 tablespoons curry powder**

- **2 tablespoons garam masala**
- **1 tablespoon seasoned salt**
- **1 teaspoon granulated sugar**
- **1 teaspoon turmeric (optional)**
- **⅛ teaspoon cayenne pepper (optional)**
- **5–8 ounces baby spinach**
- **1 cup heavy cream or half-and-half**

1 Place the butter in the Instant Pot and then hit Sauté and Adjust so it's on the More or High setting.

2 Once the butter's melted, add the onion and sauté until translucent, about 3 minutes. Add the garlic and ginger and sauté for 2 minutes longer.

3 Pour in the coconut milk and broth and deglaze (scrape) the bottom of the pot until nice and smooth. Add in the split peas, curry powder, garam masala, seasoned salt, sugar, turmeric (if using), and cayenne pepper (if using). Stir to combine.

4 Top off with the spinach, but *do not stir*—just let it rest on top.

5 Secure the lid, move the valve to the sealing position, and hit Keep Warm/Cancel followed by Manual or Pressure Cook on High Pressure for 15 minutes. When done, allow a 10-minute natural release followed by a quick release.

6 Remove the lid and stir in the cream.

7 Serve over rice, with naan, or on a bun.

JEFF'S TIPS When done, this is going to thicken quickly while setting. If you'd like it thinner (or if reheating leftovers), simply add more cream or broth just before serving.

Because people like their lentils at different textures, I'll give you some options. Natural release for:

- **5 MINUTES:** al dente, holding their form
- **10 MINUTES:** medium with a perfect bite and softer form (as recipe is written)
- **15 MINUTES:** soft, with a more mushy texture

SPAGHETTI SQUASH SCAMPI

If you're a pasta lover but have to watch your carb intake, you've just found the greatest solution ever. Spaghetti squash is exactly as it sounds—a squash that, when cooked and shredded, takes on the form of a slightly sweet, al dente spaghetti. It's delicious with this simple scampi sauce.

Prep Time	Sauté Time	Pressure Building Time	Pressure Cook Time	Total Time	Serves
5 minutes	**5** minutes	**10–15** minutes	**6** minutes	**30** minutes	**4**

1 cup water

1 (3–4-pound) spaghetti squash, halved, seeds scooped out

1 tablespoon extra-virgin olive oil

2 tablespoons (¼ stick) salted butter

2 shallots, diced

6 cloves garlic, minced or pressed

¼ cup dry white wine (like a sauvignon blanc)

Juice of 1 lemon

1 tablespoon dried parsley flakes

½ teaspoon kosher salt

½ teaspoon black pepper

¼ cup grated Parmesan cheese

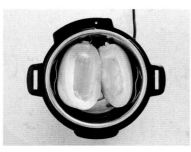

1 Place the trivet in the Instant Pot, pour in the water, and place the squash halves on the trivet, skin side-down.

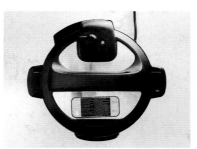

2 Secure the lid, turn the valve to the sealing position, and hit Manual or Pressure Cook on High Pressure for 6 minutes. Quick release when done.

3 Carefully remove the squash and use a fork to shred it into spaghetti.

4 Transfer the shredded squash to a bowl and discard the squash skin. Empty the liner pot and return it to the Instant Pot (no need to wash).

5 Put the olive oil and butter in the pot, hit Keep Warm/Cancel, then hit Sauté and Adjust so it's on the More or High setting. Once the butter's melted, add the shallots and cook for about 2 minutes, until beginning to brown. Add the garlic and sauté for another minute.

6 Stir in the wine, lemon juice, parsley flakes, kosher salt, and black pepper. Simmer for 1 minute.

7 Add in the shredded spaghetti squash, top with the Parmesan, toss with tongs until fully combined, and serve.

JEFF'S TIP If this sauce is too rich for you to pair with a healthy spaghetti squash, feel free to use another kind. Garlic Marinara Sauce (page 34) or pesto both go wonderfully.

PORTOBELLO POT ROAST

A portobello mushroom is the steak of the veggie world. Fork-tender, juicy, and full of flavor, this marvelous mushroom fools even the most dedicated vegetable haters. The best part? This veggie roast cooks up in just half the time of a beef roast.

Prep Time	Sauté Time	Pressure Building Time	Pressure Cook Time	Total Time	Serves
15 minutes	13 minutes	10–15 minutes	5 minutes	45 minutes	4–8

- 2 tablespoons extra-virgin olive oil
- 2 medium yellow onions, sliced into thick wedges
- 6 cloves garlic, sliced
- 6 tablespoons (¾ stick) salted butter
- 2 tablespoons Worcestershire sauce

- 2 pounds baby bella mushrooms, 1 pound left whole and 1 pound sliced
- ½ cup dry red wine (like a pinot noir)
- 1 cup mushroom broth (e.g. Mushroom Better Than Bouillon) or vegetable broth
- 1½ teaspoons dried parsley flakes
- 1½ teaspoons seasoned salt

- 2 teaspoons black pepper
- 1 teaspoon dried thyme
- 1 teaspoon dried rosemary
- 1½ pounds portobello mushroom caps, stems removed
- 1 bunch asparagus, tough ends removed
- 2 tablespoons cornstarch
- 1 mushroom gravy packet (optional)

1 Pour the oil into the Instant Pot and press Sauté and Adjust to the More or High setting. Heat the oil for 3 minutes, add the onions, and sauté for 3 minutes, until slightly softened. Add the garlic and cook for 1 minute more.

2 Add the butter and Worcestershire sauce and, once the butter is melted, add all the baby bella mushrooms and sauté for 5 minutes, until they begin to brown and cook down.

3 Pour the wine and broth over everything and add the parsley flakes, seasoned salt, black pepper, thyme, and rosemary. Stir well and then lay the portobello mushrooms on top, stacking them.

4 Gently place the asparagus on top of the mushrooms.

5 Secure the lid, move the valve to the sealing position, hit Keep Warm/Cancel, then hit Manual or Pressure Cook on High Pressure for 5 minutes. Quick release when done.

6 Meanwhile, stir the cornstarch into 2 tablespoons of cold water to form a slurry and set aside.

7 Remove the asparagus and set aside. Using a slotted spoon and tongs, carefully transfer all the mushrooms to a serving dish and rest the asparagus beside them.

8 On the Instant Pot, press Keep Warm/Cancel and then Sauté and Adjust so it's on the More or High setting, and bring the sauce to a simmer. Add the gravy packet (if using) and the cornstarch slurry, and immediately stir until combined. Allow to simmer for 30 seconds, then hit Keep Warm/Cancel to turn off the pot and allow to sit for a minute.

9 Ladle the sauce over the mushrooms and serve with crusty bread (for lapping up the sauce).

MAPLE BALSAMIC

BRUSSELS
SPROUTS

I used to not even be able to look at Brussels sprouts, let alone eat them. They just weren't my thang. After conjuring up this recipe, my, how things have changed!

Prep Time	Sauté Time	Pressure Building Time	Pressure Cook Time	Optional Oven Time	Total Time	Serves
5 minutes	**5** minutes	**5–10** minutes	**1** minute	**10–15** minutes	**35** minutes	**4–6**

2 tablespoons (¼ stick) salted butter

2 shallots, diced

2–3 pounds Brussels sprouts, stems trimmed, halved

⅓ cup balsamic vinegar

¼ cup maple syrup

1 cup dried cranberries or Craisins

10–20 almonds, crushed

Balsamic glaze, for topping (optional)

1 Place the butter in the Instant Pot and press Sauté and Adjust to the More or High setting. Once the butter's melted, add the shallots and sauté for 3 minutes, until slightly softened.

2 Add the Brussels sprouts, vinegar, maple syrup, cranberries, and almonds. Stir until everything is mixed together and the Brussels sprouts are well-coated in the sauce.

3 Secure the lid, move the valve to the sealing position, and hit Manual or Pressure Cook on High Pressure for 1 minute. Quick release when done and remove the sprouts from the Instant Pot.

JEFF'S TIP

If you have leftovers, they taste amazing cold right out of the fridge too!

4 *To crisp the sprouts (optional):* Place the Brussels sprouts on a foil-lined baking sheet in a preheated 400°F oven and roast for 10–15 minutes, until golden-brown and crispy (keep an eye on them as oven temperatures vary). Or, if you have an Instant Pot Duo Crisp, use the crisping lid and hit Air Fry at 400°F for 5–10 minutes until they reach the desired crispiness.

5 Place the Brussels sprouts in a serving dish, along with their sauce, and drizzle with some balsamic glaze, if desired.

PREMIUM POTATO SALAD

Potato salad never used to do it for me. I always found it meh compared to my true love, macaroni salad. But many of my readers asked me to make one, and I'm glad I did—because this potato salad is now the first thing I'll eat at a barbecue, even before the meat.

Prep Time	Pressure Building Time	Pressure Cook Time	Total Time	Serves
10 minutes	**5–10** minutes	**6** minutes	**30** minutes (4 hours with refrigeration time)	**4–6**

- **4 pounds potatoes, cut into large 1-inch chunks** (NOTE: I like to use 2 pounds white or Yukon Gold and 2 pounds baby red potatoes, skins on; but if using russet or Idaho potatoes, peel the skins off.)
- **5 large raw eggs in their shells**
- **2 cups mayonnaise**
- **1 cup sweet relish** (or finely chopped dill or kosher pickles if you prefer)
- **2 tablespoons Russian or Thousand Island salad dressing** (if using Russian, make sure it's the creamy, mayonnaise-based kind, not the bright-red one)
- **1 tablespoon apple cider vinegar**
- **1 tablespoon Dijon mustard**
- **1 tablespoon yellow mustard**
- **½ teaspoon paprika**
- **1½ teaspoons celery seed** (optional)
- **1 bunch scallions, thinly sliced**
- **¼ cup fresh dill, roughly chopped** (plus more for garnish, if desired)
- **½ cup real bacon pieces,** *or* **6 strips of cooked bacon, diced into small pieces** (optional)
- **1 cup (4 ounces) shredded Cheddar cheese** (optional)

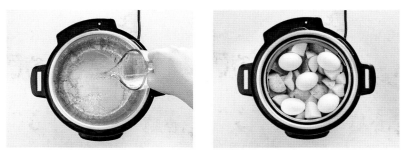

1 Pour 1 cup of water in the Instant Pot, followed by a steamer basket holding the potatoes and eggs. (NOTE: If you don't have a steamer basket, just lay the potatoes inside the liner pot and rest the eggs on top.) Gently secure the lid (making sure the eggs are clear of it), move the valve to the sealing position, and hit Manual or Pressure Cook at High Pressure for 6 minutes. Quick release when done.

2 Meanwhile, make the dressing. In a mixing bowl, stir together the mayonnaise, relish, salad dressing, vinegar, mustards, paprika, celery seed (if using), scallions, and dill. Set aside in the fridge until ready to use.

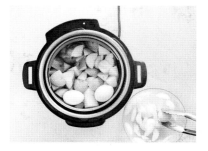

3 Prepare an ice bath by filling a large bowl halfway with ice and water.

4 Once the cooking is finished, remove the steamer basket from the Instant Pot and immediately transfer the eggs to the ice bath and let them cool for 90 seconds. Drain the potatoes in a colander if you didn't use a basket. Allow the potatoes to cool for 10–20 minutes. Peel the eggs and coarsely chop them.

5 Once the potatoes have cooled down a bit, add them to a large serving bowl, topped with the dressing along with the egg, bacon (if using), and cheese (if using) and gently toss until fully coated.

6 Place in the fridge to cool and set for 3–4 hours before serving.

JEFF'S TIP Some prefer celery in their potato salad for crunch—feel free to chop up 2 ribs of celery and add them with the scallions and dill.

RATATOUILLE STEW

Vegetarians, rejoice! Ratatouille is a rustic vegetable dish so deep in flavor, you might forget it's made of only veggies! And I've turned it into a luscious stew. This is the perfect side dish—delicious both hot or cold—or a delightful meal in itself. It tastes like a wonderful harvest in your mouth—with *zero* guilt!

Prep Time	Sauté Time	Pressure Building Time	Pressure Cook Time	Total Time	Serves
15 minutes	**7** minutes	**10–20** minutes	**2** minutes	**45** minutes	**4–6**

- ¼ cup extra-virgin olive oil
- 1 large Vidalia (sweet) onion, coarsely chopped
- 1 green bell pepper, cut into medium dice
- 1 red bell pepper, cut into medium dice
- 6 cloves garlic, minced or pressed
- 1 large eggplant, skin on, sliced into ½-inch disks and then quartered

- 1 large zucchini, skin on, cut into ¼-inch disks and then quartered
- 1 medium yellow (summer) squash, skin on, cut into ¼-inch disks and then quartered
- 1 (14.5-ounce) can diced tomatoes, drained
- 2 teaspoons Italian seasoning
- 1½ teaspoons herbes de Provence (optional)
- 1 teaspoon kosher salt

- 1 teaspoon black pepper
- ½ teaspoon dried thyme
- ½ cup vegetable broth or dry red wine (like a cabernet)
- 1 tablespoon Worcestershire sauce
- 1 (6-ounce) can of tomato paste
- Grated Parmesan cheese, for serving (optional)

1 Pour the oil into the Instant Pot and hit Sauté and Adjust so it's on the More or High setting. Heat about 3 minutes, then add the onion and bell peppers and sauté, stirring, for about 3 minutes, until they begin to soften. Add the garlic and sauté for another minute.

2 Add the other vegetables along with the Italian seasoning, herbes de Provence (if using), kosher salt, black pepper, dried thyme, vegetable broth or wine, and Worcestershire sauce.

3 Secure the lid, move the valve to the sealing position, and hit Keep Warm/Cancel, then hit Manual or Pressure Cook on High Pressure for 2 minutes.

4 Stir in in the tomato paste. Let stand for about 10 minutes before serving. Don't worry if it looks a little soupy—it will thicken as it cools down and the vegetables continue to absorb the broth. Serve with grated Parmesan cheese, if desired.

JEFF'S TIP It'll feel like you're putting an entire garden into the Instant Pot with little liquid. But veggies release a bunch of water under pressure. This is what causes this dish to cook down and makes it such a comforting stew.

SZECHUAN STRING BEANS

If you ever thought green beans were boring, you'll find these spicy, mouthwatering ones are a whole lotta interesting.

Prep Time	Pressure Building Time	Pressure Cook Time	Total Time	Serves
5 minutes	**5–10** minutes	**3** minutes	**20** minutes	**4–6**

1½ pounds green beans, ends trimmed

¼ cup vegetable or garlic broth (e.g. Garlic Better Than Bouillon)

¼ cup low-sodium soy sauce

2 tablespoons almonds, chopped (optional)

3 cloves garlic, minced or pressed

2 tablespoons sesame oil

2 tablespoons sriracha

1 tablespoon rice vinegar

1 tablespoon paprika

2 teaspoons garlic powder

1 teaspoon onion powder

¼ teaspoon cayenne pepper (optional)

¼ teaspoon crushed red pepper flakes (optional)

1 Put all the ingredients in the Instant Pot and stir well.

2 Secure the lid, move the valve to the sealing position, and hit Manual or Pressure Cook on High Pressure for 3 minutes. Quick release when done.

3 When the lid comes off, you're ready to serve.

JEFF'S TIPS Using sriracha, cayenne, and crushed red pepper flakes will make this dish fairly spicy. If you want it milder, start with a smaller amount of sriracha and add more to taste. Skip or reduce the amount of the cayenne and pepper flakes.

REFRIED BEANS

Can beans really be magic? Just ask Jack what happened with his. While these Refried Beans won't make beanstalks stretch to the skies, they certainly carry a magic of their own—creamy flavor that will complete any Mexican meal. Try them with my White Queso Chicken Enchilada Casserole (page 144) or Arroz con Pollo (page 110).

Prep Time	Sauté Time	Pressure Building Time	Pressure Cook Time	Natural Release Time	Total Time	Serves
5 minutes	8 minutes	10–20 minutes	35 minutes	30 minutes	100 minutes	4–6

¼ cup vegetable oil

1 large Spanish (or yellow) onion, diced

3 cloves garlic, minced or pressed

4 ounces canned green chilies, with their juices

5 cups water or garlic broth (e.g. Garlic Better Than Bouillon, for more flavor)

2 cups dried pinto beans (not canned), rinsed and drained

1½ teaspoons kosher salt, divided

3 bay leaves

1 teaspoon seasoned salt

1¼ cups crumbled cotija cheese (use crumbled feta or grated Parmesan if you can't find cotija)

1 Pour the oil into the Instant Pot and hit Sauté and Adjust so it's on the High or More setting. Heat for 3 minutes, then add the onion, garlic, and green chilies. Give it all a good stir and then let it cook, stirring occasionally, until softened and very fragrant, about 5 minutes.

2 Add the water or broth and stir, scraping up any browned bits from the bottom of the pot. Add the pinto beans, 1 teaspoon of the kosher salt, and the bay leaves.

3 Secure the lid, move the valve to the sealing position, hit Keep Warm/Cancel and then hit Manual or Pressure Cook on High Pressure for 35 minutes. When done, allow a 30-minute natural release and follow with a quick release.

4 When the lid comes off, discard the bay leaves. Don't worry if the beans appear a little watery. Leaving everything in the pot, use a potato masher to mash the beans to the desired consistency. The starchy innards of the beans will thicken the dish, and the more/harder the mashing, the less chunky and smoother the beans will be.

5 Stir in the remaining ½ teaspoon of kosher salt, seasoned salt, and cotija cheese and serve.

 JEFF'S TIPS The beans will thicken as they cool, so if you want to make sure yours are thickened to your liking, you can remove some of the liquid with a serving spoon before mashing the beans and then add some of it back afterward.

If you want your refried beans smooth, puree them with an immersion blender right in the pot just before serving.

ROASTED RED PEPPER HUMMUS

The Instant Pot truly can do wonders. Just try this amazing homemade hummus, and you'll know why. This healthy dip is great with pita chips, or in my Chicken Shawarma (page 142).

Prep Time	Pressure Building Time	Pressure Cook Time	Natural Release Time	Total Time	Serves
10 minutes	**10–20** minutes	**20** minutes	**5** minutes	**60** minutes (10 hours with soaking and refrigeration time)	**4–6**

1 cup dried chickpeas (garbanzo beans)

3½ cups vegetable broth

6 cloves garlic, minced or pressed

1 bay leaf

Juice of 1 lemon

3 tablespoons tahini (sesame paste)

2 tablespoons extra-virgin olive oil, plus more for drizzling

1 teaspoon cumin

1 teaspoon seasoned salt

1 teaspoon garlic salt

1 (7-ounce) jar roasted red peppers, divided and juice reserved

Any other of your favorite seasonings, to taste

1 Place the chickpeas in a large pot or mixing bowl, add about 4 cups of hot water, and cover. Allow to soak at room temperature for 8 hours. (NOTE: Do not skip this step!)

2 After soaking, drain and rinse the chickpeas in a strainer. Place them in the Instant Pot along with the broth, garlic, and bay leaf.

3 Secure the lid, move the valve to the sealing position, and hit Manual or Pressure Cook on High Pressure for 20 minutes. When done, allow a 5-minute natural release followed by a quick release.

4 Discard the bay leaf and reserve ½ cup of the cooking liquid before straining the chickpeas.

JEFF'S TIPS Want it a little spicy? Add a tablespoon of sriracha and/or about ¼ tablespoon crushed red pepper flakes before blending.

Don't like red peppers? Leave them out and make it plain!

5 In a food processor or blender, combine the chickpeas, lemon juice, tahini, olive oil, cumin, seasoned salt, garlic salt, half of the roasted red peppers and a few splashes of juice from the jar, and the reserved cooking liquid. Pulse and then blend until creamy, scraping down the sides halfway through. Add seasonings of your choice to taste.

6 Pop in the fridge to cool for 2 hours. Meanwhile, roughly chop the remaining peppers for garnish.

7 When you're ready to serve, use a spoon to carve a little crater in the center of the hummus and fill with the remaining red peppers. At the table, drizzle some olive oil over the top.

CAULIFLOWER PUREE

I have a confession: I used to hate many of the veggies used in this book, but preparing these delicious recipes has made me a believer. If you're a cauliflower hater but love creamy mashed potatoes, trust me: try this recipe.

Prep Time	Pressure Building Time	Pressure Cook Time	Total Time	Serves
5 minutes	**5–10** minutes	**4** minutes	**20** minutes	**4–6**

- **1 cup chicken or vegetable broth**
- **1 head cauliflower, stalk and green leaves removed, cut into large chunks**
- **½ cup milk, heavy cream, or half-and-half**
- **2 tablespoons (¼ stick) salted butter**
- **Seasoned salt and black pepper to taste**
- **Chopped chives, for garnish**

1 Place the trivet in the Instant Pot, pour in the broth, and place the cauliflower on top.

2 Secure the lid, move the valve to the sealing position, and hit Manual or Pressure Cook on High Pressure for 4 minutes. Quick release when done.

3 Transfer the cauliflower to a food processor or blender. Pour in about a third of the broth from the pot. Pulse and then blend to form a smooth puree.

4 Add the milk, butter, seasoned salt, and pepper to the blender. Pulse and blend again until totally smooth and creamy before serving with some chives, perhaps.

JEFF'S TIP If you want to use other seasonings, go wild! This dish is your canvas. The sky's the limit!

CRABBY CREAMED CORN

This is, by far, the most decadent creamed corn I've ever had—and it's always the first side dish to disappear from the table. In fact, you may want to double this recipe no matter what. Oh, and you're going to laugh at how easy and quick it is to make.

Prep Time	Pressure Building Time	Pressure Cook Time	Total Time	Serves
3 minutes	**5–10** minutes	**1** minute	**15** minutes	**4–6**

1   cup water

30   ounces frozen corn

½   pound lump crabmeat or 2 (6-ounce) cans white or pink crabmeat, drained

1   (5.2-ounce) package Boursin spread (any flavor) or 4 ounces cream cheese, cut into chunky cubes

½   cup heavy cream or half-and-half

½   cup grated Parmesan cheese

3   tablespoons salted butter

1½   teaspoons granulated sugar

1   teaspoon black pepper

1 Pour the water in the Instant Pot then place the corn in a steamer basket and lower into the pot.

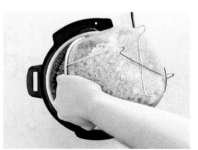

2 Secure the lid, move the valve to the sealing position, and hit Manual or Pressure Cook on High Pressure for 1 minute. Quick release when done. Lift the liner from the pot to drain and return it to the Instant Pot. Dump the corn from the basket back into the pot.

3 Add all the other ingredients and stir until the Boursin (or cream cheese) has melted completely before serving.

JEFF'S TIP

Want to make it a casserole? Transfer the finished creamed corn to a casserole dish. Then mix together about 1 cup of crushed **Ritz** crackers and 4 tablespoons (½ stick) melted butter to form a crust. Top the creamed corn with the crust and place in the oven to broil for a few minutes until browned (keep an eye on it, as oven temperatures vary). You can also do this in an Instant Pot Duo Crisp by using the crisping lid and hitting Bake at 400°F for 5–10 minutes.

9

DESSERT

Like I'd close this book without giving you
a sweet sendoff? As shocking as it may seem, the Instant Pot is a pro
at cooking desserts. And that goes as much for desserts
made directly in the pot, like Apple Crumble Cobbler, as for
pot-in-pot recipes like Cheesecake or Crème Brûlée.
Whatever you choose to make, your Instant Pot will help you
create a luscious ending to a beautiful day.

Crème Brûlée
252

**Apple Crumble
Cobbler**
254

Bananas Foster
256

**Customizable
Cheesecake**
258

**Lemon Ginger
Blueberry Cake**
260

**Peanut Butter
Fudge Cookie
Dough Tart**
262

CRÈME BRÛLÉE

Let's go skating on a decadent custard with a crust. Not only is this one of the best Crème Brûlées I've ever cracked the surface of, it's one of the easiest to make. You'll need four 8-ounce oven-safe ramekins for this one.

Prep Time	Pressure Building Time	Pressure Cook Time	Natural Release Time	Total Time	Serves
5 minutes	**5–10** minutes	**15** minutes	**15** minutes	**45** minutes (5 hours with refrigeration time)	**4**

THE CUSTARD
- 2 cups heavy cream
- 6 egg yolks
- 6 tablespoons granulated sugar
- ⅛ teaspoon nutmeg
- ⅛ teaspoon cinnamon
- 1½ teaspoons vanilla extract

THE CRUST
- ¼ cup granulated white or raw sugar (1 tablespoon per ramekin)

1 Pour the cream into a 4-cup Pyrex or medium microwave-safe bowl and microwave for 45 seconds.

2 Whisk the egg yolks, sugar, nutmeg, cinnamon, and vanilla into the warmed cream.

3 Divide the mixture into four 8-ounce ceramic ramekins and cover each with foil.

4 Place the trivet in the Instant Pot with 2 cups of water.

5 Rest the ramekins on top of the trivet in two layers in crisscross fashion.

6 Secure the lid, move the valve to the sealing position, and hit Manual or Pressure Cook on High Pressure for 15 minutes. When done, allow a 15-minute natural release followed by a quick release. Before removing the ramekins, allow them to cool for 5 minutes in the pot.

7 Remove the foil. The custard will appear a little jiggly, like Jell-O. Place the ramekins in the fridge for at least 4 hours, preferably overnight, until firm and like pudding in consistency.

8 When ready to serve, evenly sprinkle each ramekin with 1 tablespoon of sugar and very carefully, in circular motions, use a culinary torch or your broiler to caramelize the top to the hue of your liking, then serve.

 JEFF'S TIPS A culinary torch is a surprisingly affordable kitchen tool—but always use caution when playing with fire in your kitchen.

Is it the holidays? Sub ½ cup eggnog for ½ cup of the cream. Just make sure you serve it under some mistletoe, because someone's gonna kiss you for making this!

APPLE CRUMBLE COBBLER

My take on this classic all-American dessert was featured on *Good Morning America* and is a crowd-pleaser for all. Whether you're cozied up by a roaring fire as the snow falls or you took your Instant Pot with you on a camping trip, apples and spice make everything nice.

Prep Time	Pressure Building Time	Pressure Cook Time	Natural Release	Total Time	Serves
10 minutes	**5–10** minutes	**2** minutes	**Full** (20–30 minutes)	**45** minutes	**4**

5   Granny Smith apples, cored, peeled, and cut into 1-inch cubes, at room temperature

2   teaspoons ground cinnamon

½   teaspoon ground nutmeg

2   tablespoons maple syrup

2   tablespoons caramel syrup (plus more for topping at the end)

½   cup water

4   tablespoons (½ stick) salted butter

⅓   cup light-brown sugar

¾   cup old-fashioned oats (not the instant kind)

¼   cup all-purpose flour

½   teaspoon sea salt

Vanilla ice cream, for serving

1 Place the apples in the Instant Pot and top with the cinnamon, nutmeg, maple syrup, caramel syrup, and water. Stir together well until a liquid consistency is reached and the apples are coated.

2 Create the topping: In a microwave-safe bowl, melt the butter, then add the brown sugar, oats, flour, and salt. Mix well and pour over the apple mixture in the pot.

3 Secure the lid, move the valve to the sealing position, and hit Manual or Pressure Cook on High Pressure for 2 minutes. When done, allow a full natural release (this will take 20–30 minutes).

4 Serve right out of the pot, topped with vanilla ice cream and some more caramel sauce, if desired.

This recipe works perfectly in a 6-quart Instant Pot, but if making in the 8-quart, be sure to double it. We aren't adding a whole lot of liquid as written and the extra circumference of the larger pot may have issues coming to pressure.

Want more of that amazing topping? Double the butter, flour, oats, brown sugar, and salt.

If you want to give it some crisping and you have the Instant Pot Duo Crisp, add the crisping lid and hit **Air Fry at 400°F for 5 minutes** before serving.

BANANAS FOSTER

I'm not monkeying around when I tell you that this boozy and brilliant dessert will have you pounding your chest and swinging from a vine. A brown-sugary, rum-infused sauce cascading over softened bananas and topped with vanilla ice cream... I'll just stop before you eat the page out of this book.

Prep Time	Pressure Building Time	Pressure Cook Time	Natural Release Time	Total Time	Serves
5 minutes	**5–10** minutes	**2** minutes	**5** minutes	**20** minutes	**4**

8 tablespoons (1 stick) salted butter, cubed	1 cup dark-brown sugar, packed	6 good-sized bananas, firm but not green, peeled and sliced into 1-inch pieces
¼ cup light (clear) rum	1 teaspoon cinnamon	
¼ cup water	1 teaspoon vanilla extract	Vanilla ice cream, for serving

1 In the Instant Pot, combine the butter, rum, water, brown sugar, cinnamon, and vanilla. Mix well until the large lumps of the sugar are dissolved and the mixture is the texture of molasses. The butter should remain chunky.

2 Add the bananas and stir gently to coat with the sauce.

3 Secure the lid, move the valve to the sealing position, and hit Manual or Pressure Cook on High Pressure for 2 minutes. When done, allow a 5-minute natural release followed by a quick release.

4 Let cool for a few moments before serving over bowls of vanilla ice cream.

 JEFF'S TIP **Bananas Foster goes *perfectly* over bread pudding, French toast, pancakes, and even cheesecake.**

CUSTOMIZABLE CHEESECAKE

I think it's important to have options in life, and this simple and astounding Customizable Cheesecake is going to let you do it your way. Boasting a buttery graham-cracker crust and baked to sheer, gorgeous perfection, this cheesecake is going to have four women living together in Miami come knocking. Don't skip softening your ingredients to room temperature before starting!

Prep Time	Pressure Building Time	Pressure Cook Time	Natural Release Time	Total Time	Serves
25 minutes	**5–10** minutes	**45** minutes	**30** minutes	**2** hours (7 hours with refrigeration time)	**6–8**

4 tablespoons (½ stick) salted butter, melted (plus more for greasing the pan)

1 cup graham cracker crumbs

2 (8-ounce) bricks of cream cheese, at room temperature (a must)

¾ cup granulated sugar

½ cup sour cream, at room temperature (also a must)

1 tablespoon all-purpose flour

1 (3.4-ounce) package Vanilla Jell-O Instant Pudding (it *must* be instant)

1½ teaspoons vanilla extract

½ teaspoon almond extract

2 large eggs, at room temperature (you get the picture)

Any cookies, candy, fruit, or topping you wish (optional)

1 Generously grease a 7 x 3-inch springform pan all over with butter, then line the bottom with a 7-inch parchment paper round and grease the top of the parchment paper as well.

2 To make the crust, mix together the graham cracker crumbs and melted butter in a bowl. Add the crust mixture to the bottom of the greased pan and, using the bottom of a drinking glass, flatten the crust so it's even on the bottom and slightly climbs the sides of the pan. Pop in the freezer for at least 15 minutes to set.

3 Using a stand mixer with the paddle attached or a hand mixer (don't try this by hand, kids), beat the cream cheese on low speed until smooth and creamy. Then, while the mixer is still running, add in this order: the sugar, sour cream, flour, pudding mix, flavor extracts, and eggs (one at a time). Keep mixing on low speed until super thick and creamy and no lumps remain, about 1 minute.

4 Take out the pan from the freezer. Spoon in the batter, leaving about ½ inch of room from the brim of the pan. Smooth the top with a spatula and cover with aluminum foil.

5 Pour 2 cups of water in the Instant Pot. Place the pan on the trivet and use the handles to carefully lower it into the pot. Secure the lid, move the valve to the sealing position, and hit Manual or Pressure Cook on High Pressure for 45 minutes. Allow a full natural release when done (which will take about 30 more minutes). Hit Keep Warm/Cancel to turn off.

6 Carefully remove the pan from the Instant Pot, remove the foil, and let sit on the trivet on the counter to cool for 30 minutes (it should be slightly jiggly when it comes out). Then, place in the fridge, still in the springform pan, and let sit for *at least* 5 hours. (NOTE: Seriously, don't even think of touching it before then as it needs steady chilling to set.)

7 When ready to serve, use a sharp knife to separate the edges from the sides of the pan, and slowly open the latch of the springform pan.

8 Top the cheesecake however you wish and serve!

 JEFF'S TIPS Top the cheesecake with any pie filling, preserves, cookies, candy, or sweet spread. There are no rules—get creative!

The crust can also be made out of crushed **Oreos** if subbed for the graham crackers in Step 2.

LEMON GINGER
BLUEBERRY CAKE

This one is for when you have no time to be bothered but want a quick and amazing dessert. Moist and delightful, this cake is not only filled with blueberries, it's finished with a simple yet decadent glaze.

Prep Time	Pressure Building Time	Pressure Cook Time	Total Time	Serves
5 minutes	**5–10** minutes	**50** minutes	**65** minutes (95 minutes with cooling time)	**6–8**

1 box lemon cake mix

⅓ cup vegetable oil

3 large eggs

1 cup ginger ale or ginger beer (for a more intense ginger flavor) or 1 cup water (if you don't want a ginger flavor)

1 cup fresh blueberries

GLAZE

1 cup confectioners' (powdered) sugar

2 tablespoons (¼ stick) unsalted butter

½ teaspoon lemon or vanilla extract

Zest of 1 lemon (optional)

JEFF'S TIP This makes for a wonderfully moist, rich cake. Goes great with some hot tea or coffee and gossip!

1 In a mixing bowl, place the cake mix, oil, eggs, and ginger ale or beer. Beat with a hand (or stand) mixer until no lumps remain.

2 Generously spray the entire inside of a 6-cup Bundt pan (which will fit your 6- or 8-quart Instant Pot) with nonstick cooking spray and then pour the batter into it, making sure not to overfill it (you may have some extra batter, which you can discard). Add the blueberries and let them rest on top of the batter (they will sink in as it bakes).

3 Cover with aluminum foil and puncture a hole down the center of the Bundt opening for steam to pass through.

4 Add 2 cups water to the Instant Pot followed by the trivet. Rest the Bundt pan on the trivet, secure the lid, move the valve to the sealing position, and hit Manual or Pressure Cook at High Pressure for 50 minutes. Quick release when done, remove from the pot, remove the foil, and allow to cool for 30 minutes sitting on the trivet on the counter.

5 About 30 minutes before you're ready to serve, make the glaze. Sift the sugar over a large mixing bowl. Separately microwave the butter for 20 seconds until melted. Add the melted butter, 2 tablespoons warm water (use 3 for it to be very thin), the extract, and lemon zest (if using) to the mixing bowl and whisk/beat until totally smooth, forming an icy-glaze consistency.

6 When ready to serve, make sure the cake is detached from the walls of the pan using a knife. Then, place a plate on top of the Bundt pan and do a quick and careful flip, gently tapping the pan so the cake slides out. Drizzle the glaze over it, top with more fresh blueberries if desired, and serve.

PEANUT BUTTER FUDGE
COOKIE DOUGH
TART

When it comes to dessert, there are three things I can never turn down: anything to do with fudge, peanut butter, or cookie dough. Why not make all three into a delightfully moist and dense tart? This dessert is absolutely outrageous, decadent, and fudgy. What's more, you can make it without ever turning on your oven.

Prep Time	Pressure Building Time	Pressure Cook Time	Natural Release Time	Total Time	Serves
10 minutes	**5–10** minutes	**25** minutes	**5** minutes	**60** minutes (2 hours with rest time)	**4–6**

1   cup granulated sugar
5   tablespoons unsalted butter
2   tablespoons smooth peanut butter
1   tablespoon vegetable oil

⅓   cup unsweetened cocoa powder
2   tablespoons water
2   teaspoons vanilla extract
2   large eggs
1   cup all-purpose flour
1   teaspoon baking powder

½   teaspoon salt
½   cup peanut butter chips
¼   cup chocolate chips
5   ounces store-bought chocolate chip cookie dough, rolled into teaspoon-size balls

1 Place the sugar, butter, and peanut butter in a microwave-safe bowl and microwave for 90 seconds. Add the vegetable oil and whisk until combined. Whisk in the cocoa powder, water, and vanilla extract. Whisk in the eggs, followed by the flour, baking powder, and salt. Stir in the two kinds of chips and set aside.

2 Generously spray the sides and bottom of a 7 x 3-inch springform pan with nonstick cooking spray. Line the bottom with parchment paper, and spray that too.

3 Pour the batter into the pan and use a spatula to level the top. Arrange the cookie-dough balls and lightly push them into the batter so they're still visible on the surface.

4 Pour 2 cups of water in the Instant Pot. Place the pan on the trivet (no need to cover with foil) and use the handles to carefully lower it into the Instant Pot.

5 Secure the lid, move the valve to the sealing position, and hit Manual or Pressure Cook on High Pressure for 25 minutes. Allow a 5-minute natural release, followed by a quick release.

6 Carefully remove the pan and trivet from the Instant Pot and let cool for 1 hour, resting the pan on the trivet on the counter. When ready to serve, carefully use a knife to cut the edges of the tart away from the pan before slowly unlatching and opening the springform pan. If you're not serving right away, keep in the refrigerator until ready to serve.

 JEFF'S TIPS If you want it to be very fudgy, chill in the fridge for 2–3 hours before serving.

We aren't using the **Cake** preset button because it doesn't know exactly what sort of "cake" we're making. Using the manual/custom setting means this tart comes out perfectly every time.

ACKNOWLEDGMENTS

This is the part of the book that makes me feel like some fancy author.

First off, I need to thank my mom and dad for their unwavering support and belief in me from day one. You are simply the greatest, most protective parents in this galaxy and I love you for it (even if it makes me grumpy sometimes).

To my amazing sister, Amanda, foodie brother-in-law David, handsome nephew Levi and beautiful niece, Stevie—you keep me wanting to try making new things for the family and help keep me young every time I see you.

To my wonderful, patient, and sweet-as-a-Southern-peach Richard. You're my rock, my best friend, and my darlin'. Thank you infinitely for your admirable patience as I took over our home while developing, writing, and photographing this book. You're everything to me and then some.

To Grandma Lil for being the person I most emanate in my family. You were always my hero and I hope that wherever in the cosmos you are, you're living it up with your stuffed cabbage, a table of some cronies to gossip with and smiling down at your Jeffala.

To my editor, Michael Szczerban, and associate editor, Nicky Guerreiro, over at Voracious/Little, Brown for contacting me to make this book, aligning on my vision for it, and believing in me that I could make it in record time (we need a drink). It's gorgeous, and I couldn't be prouder of it thanks to your sensational tenacity.

To my copy editor, Peggy Freudenthal, for making me look grammatically sharp and cookbook lingo brilliant, and to Jayne Yaffe Kemp and Pat Jalbert-Levine, for shepherding this book through the tricky editorial and production stages.

To my literary agent, Nicole Tourtelot, at DeFiore and Co. Your guidance, encouragement and brilliance has made this process sane and well worth every second.

To Eric & Meredith Simonoff for connecting me with Nicole.

To Laura Palese, for making this book look so beautiful and fun. (Google her to see some of the big deal cookbooks she designed!)

To Carla Bushey, for predicting this would become my future and for generously showing me some very valuable ropes along the way.

To the extraordinary Lexi Zozulya for being the photographical force behind each and every absolutely stunning and mouthwatering photo you see in this book. And to the magical Sarah Constantino, for being the ultimate food stylist and making my creations look extra gorgeous on the plate. There are no other people I'd rather be stuck in a room with for twenty (long) days. Through all the madness, it was worth every second.

To my close friends who were always supportive of me on this journey (you know who you are). I love you like family.

But most importantly, I need to thank all of you reading this book (especially if you've made it this far). Just over two years ago, I was in a job that made me feel trapped with nowhere to go. When I started Pressure Luck as a simple creative outlet for myself, never in my wildest dreams did I think it would become my new career. It is because of each and every one of you that this book is in your hands and I shall never, ever forget it.

INDEX